Opening the Red Door

Opening the Red Door

Pastoral Counseling for Second-Generation
Korean Americans in Third Space

Hae-Jin Choe

◆PICKWICK *Publications* · Eugene, Oregon

OPENING THE RED DOOR
Pastoral Counseling for Second-Generation Korean Americans in Third Space

Copyright © 2022 Hae-Jin Choe. All rights reserved. Except for brief quotations in critical publications or reviews, no part of this book may be reproduced in any manner without prior written permission from the publisher. Write: Permissions, Wipf and Stock Publishers, 199 W. 8th Ave., Suite 3, Eugene, OR 97401.

Pickwick Publications
An Imprint of Wipf and Stock Publishers
199 W. 8th Ave., Suite 3
Eugene, OR 97401

www.wipfandstock.com

PAPERBACK ISBN: 978-1-6667-1116-5
HARDCOVER ISBN: 978-1-6667-1117-2
EBOOK ISBN: 978-1-6667-1118-9

Cataloguing-in-Publication data:

Names: Choe, Hae-Jin, author.

Title: Opening the red door : pastoral counseling for second-generation Korean Americans in third space / Hae-Jin Choe.

Description: Eugene, OR : Pickwick Publications, 2022 | Includes bibliographical references and index.

Identifiers: ISBN 978-1-6667-1116-5 (paperback) | ISBN 978-1-6667-1117-2 (hardcover) | ISBN 978-1-6667-1118-9 (ebook)

Subjects: LCSH: Church work with Korean Americans. | Pastoral counseling. | Pastoral care-United States.

Classification: BV4468.2.K6 C48 2022 (print) | BV4468.2.K6 C48 (ebook)

04/11/22

Unless otherwise indicated, Scripture quotations are from New Revised Standard Version Bible, copyright © 1989 National Council of the Churches of Christ in the United States of America. Used by permission. All rights reserved worldwide.

Contents

Acknowledgments | vii
Abbreviations | ix

Introduction | 1
    Why Red Door Ministry: Origins and Nomenclature | 2
    A Small Sample with Limitless Knowledge: The Other Three Clients | 4
    Framing the Door: Methods of Research | 6
    The Researcher and the Participants | 7
    A Walk through the Red Door: Chapter Outline | 9

1 **Red Door Ministry in Context** | 11
    In Search of Home | 11
    Double Lives | 14
    Mental Health Consequences of Double Lives | 29
    The Double Life of The Korean American Church | 34
    Homecoming: Red Door Ministry as a Place for Wholeness | 39

2 **The Space of Red Door Ministry** | 42
    Defining Space | 42
    Postcolonial Theory: Creating a Third Space | 43
    Imagined Space to Physical Space | 52
    Counselor's Inner Space | 58

3 **What Happens in Red Door Ministry** | 70
    Western vs. Eastern View of Self | 71
    Shame and SGKAs | 73
    Western Psychological Theorists | 82
    Eastern Theorists | 95
    Beyond Shame | 107

4 **Transformations in Red Door Ministry: Theological Implications** | 110
    Red Door Ministry Six Step Transformation Model: From Margins to New Centers | 111
    Step 1: Opening and Embracing Possibilities | 112
    Step 2: Identifying Oppressive Systems | 114
    Step 3: Identifying Redemptive Elements | 117
    Step 4: Using Redemptive Elements to Challenge Oppressive Systems | 122
    Step 5: Owning Power and Agency | 126
    Step 6: Co-Creating New Centers | 131
    The Flow of Divine Movement | 136

5 **Going Beyond the Red Door Ministry** | 138
    The Clients: Beyond the Red Door Ministry | 139
    The Community: Beyond the Red Door Ministry | 143
    The Caregiver: Beyond the Red Door Ministry | 148

Appendix: Interview Questions | 151
Bibliography | 155
Index | 161

Acknowledgments

I WOULD LIKE TO express my deep gratitude to all the clients who have come to Red Door Ministry since it opened its doors in 2016. Allowing me to join in their journey towards healing, growth and empowerment have added much to my own. Their courage and transformation have been an inspiration for me. A special thank you to the four clients who graciously volunteered to share their experiences for this book.

To the professors, colleagues and spiritual companions who have helped me find my voice. My deep gratitude to Gregory Ellison, Emmanuel Lartey, Carolyn McCrary, and Bill Harkins.

To Joan Murray who have walked with me as a faithful spiritual friend for over a decade.

To Jina Kim, my dear friend who fed my stomach and my soul on countless occasions bringing color and life to this process. I cannot imagine being without her support and friendship.

To my beloved family; my mother, Ae Joo for her daily prayers; my sister, Hae-Rin for listening and reading my ideas into being; my brother-in-law, Eugene for his support and theological conversations; my nephews, William and Theodore for making me smile and laugh when I desperately needed it; and my father David whose life and death laid a foundation for my own life to flourish.

Abbreviations

RDM   Red Door Ministry

SGKA/SGKAs   Second-Generation Korean American/s

Introduction

"[I HAD] FEELINGS OF non-existing . . . it was getting worse and worse and I just felt desperate to feel something,"[1] said Ava, a twenty-six-year-old Korean American woman. This was her answer when asked for her reasons for entering the counseling space of Red Door Ministry (hereafter abbreviated to RDM). Her feelings stemmed from the constant drum of anxiously racing thoughts. In her efforts to block out these racing thoughts, Ava ultimately disconnected herself from living life and numbed herself from her feelings. Seeking a path out of anxiety, Ava arrived at RDM, a pastoral counseling space in a Korean American church, after years of receiving counseling from several different counselors with little improvement in her symptoms. Although hesitant to give counseling another try, she arrived, out of desperation, wanting to cling onto anything that made her feel connected to herself and the people around her. In the months that I counseled Ava, we paused, reflected, and worked together to unfold some of the reasons for her anxiety. Through self-compassion, understanding, and critique of the source of her anxiety, Ava created room to hear her own voice and value it. She described her transformation and growth from over a year's work as "magic." In her reflections on the "magic" of RDM, Ava shared that the space "gives me a break . . . from life . . . [that] makes you stop and think."[2]

1. Ava, interview by author, July 5, 2017.
2. Ava, interview by author, July 5, 2017.

Given Ava's long history and lack of resolution with previous counselors, what was different about the care she received from RDM? What were the elements that were unique to this space that allowed Ava to reclaim her life? How did the counselor/caregiver at RDM assume a culturally relevant and context-sensitive posture that was highly conducive to addressing the needs of second-generation Korean Americans? This book will explore the cultural origins and theoretical influences that make RDM a substantive model for the field of pastoral care and counseling and provide a template for church-based counseling centers.

Why Red Door Ministry: Origins and Nomenclature

RDM first opened its doors in January 2016 as a pastoral care and counseling center at a local Korean American church. This space was created to address the needs of second-generation Korean Americans (hereafter abbreviated to SGKAs) and their families. The mission statement of RDM is "Creating a safe place for *truth* to be revealed, where *healing* and *peace* take place in new life." In the past five years, over ninety people, both first-generation Korean Americans and SGKAs, have entered individually, as couples, or with family members to embark on a journey of self-discovery, freedom, and empowerment. I chose the name *Red Door* to symbolize the blood of Christ, through whom sins are forgiven and brokenness embraced. As in the Passover when God's judgment passed over the Israelites because of the blood on the door, I pray that all who enter RDM find safety within its walls. I further stress that every person entering RDM is cared for as a child of God who is created in God's image. To be sure, this passage can also evoke images of God's violence and the blood required to appease God's judgment. I stress, however, that the blood acts as an embrace and cover for the deep stains of sin and brokenness. Theological reflection on the events in RDM will be discussed in greater detail in chapter 4.

What makes RDM a *pastoral* counseling center? Is pastoral counseling still a relevant method of care in the increasingly intercultural and interfaith zeitgeist that defines our time? The recent movement of changing the names of many *pastoral* care departments to *spiritual* care departments shows a departure from a strictly Christian focus to an embracing of a more pluralistic spirituality in the care of souls. This movement of changing names has also been true of counseling. With a steady openness toward the spiritual dimension, psychologists and counselors are making room for a

Introduction

client's spirituality in their interventions. Counselors, whether secularly or pastorally trained, can no longer ignore the need for an inclusive attitude for the diverse spiritual beliefs their clients hold and practice. So why not call RDM a place of spiritual counseling?

I have retained the nomenclature of *pastoral* care and counseling to emphasize the theories and practices of the field that are being used within RDM. Although the clients are given the choice of whether they would prefer to engage in counseling with their faith and spirituality as part of the process or to maintain a strictly secular route, my view and framework as the counselor for each client is one of *pastoral* counselor. I cannot separate my beliefs that each human being is created in God's image to live a life of freedom, hope, and empowerment. God may seldom be mentioned in the room by name, but my faith and hope in God, who makes all things new, undergirds each session I hold with clients.

RDM is also a place for critically examining oppressive forces that have suppressed the voices of the clients who enter. Formed with a postcolonial perspective from its inception, this space aims to create new centers for those who have been placed on the margins. In this study, as the relationship between *center* and *margins* is re-evaluated, center[3] needs to be further defined. By *center*, I mean the *space* where people are empowered to live as complex human beings whose experiences and contributions are seen and valued by society. RDM utilizes the concept of *third space* from Homi Bhabha as a base of reaching this newly defined center. A detailed look at how the postcolonial lens contributes to the formation of this space will follow in chapter 2.

RDM reflects my own journey toward freedom and empowerment. In this regard, RDM pays homage to the many guides who have walked before me and with me. Years before RDM was founded, I envisioned recreating a space similar to the places on my personal journey where I found freedom and voice. To this end, RDM draws upon the wisdom of spiritual directors, therapists, supervisors, professors, and friends who have helped me discern my own voice. Through this hybridity of wisdom, I have been able to put into practice diverse skills and theories that I have learned from a host of teachers. My aim is that this knowledge and those skills gained in

---

3. Traditionally, the word *center* has been used to refer to the social, cultural, political, and racial location of those in the dominant group (historically that group has been mostly Western, White, and male) who have pushed those outside the group to the margins. Those who are excluded from this center or marginalized have been devalued, objectified, and stereotyped by those in the center.

my studies and training as a pastoral counselor might be employed at RDM to launch others on their own paths of transformation.

Spaces such as RDM are rare because they bring together various factors such as cultural awareness and sensitivity, postcolonial thought, psychological theories, and pastoral theological practice to provide relevant, holistic care for a specific group of people. In this case, the cultural elements and the specific population refer to the SGKAs in the southeastern United States who live in the constant flux of moving between Korean and American cultures. By taking elements from various fields, RDM pieces together a new mosaic from seemingly different scraps. This "scrappy" work of creating has not always been easy. Adopting a self-critical stance as a counselor grounds me in this messy ordeal of piecing together the scraps for the greater good. It has been helpful to remain ever open and flexible and to not take myself too seriously as I make more room for this amalgam to form. A new metaphor of *fusion chef*[4] for the development of this space of intercultural pastoral care has given me guidance and courage to combine various factors to form this space. As more SGKA clients enter the innovative space of RDM to reclaim their voices, a thorough description and evaluation of the elements involved within it seemed worthwhile. This study focuses on the clients' voices for their personal telling of their journey from desperation and despair to a place of hope, empowerment, and wisdom.

A Small Sample with Limitless Knowledge: The Other Three Clients

The voices of four SGKAs from RDM are used to explore the contexts and elements that make transformation possible. Although four is a seemingly small sample size for generalization, the experiences of these four clients highlight psychological and theological themes and shared life circumstances of other clients who have seen positive changes during their time in RDM. The words of these four clients will be woven throughout the chapters to offer contextual analysis, to provide connection to larger theories, and to examine why specific practices of care were used in RDM to assist in their transformation. Each of these four clients have participated in at least ten counseling sessions; some have attended as many as forty sessions by the time they were interviewed. Through these sessions, the

---

4. The origins and details of this metaphor will be explored in chapter 3.

Introduction

four clients have undergone noticeable changes in their mental, emotional, and spiritual health. Ava, Jason, Sam and Rose, all pseudonyms they have chosen, have graciously agreed to share their experiences of RDM. A brief introduction will help the reader get acquainted with their voices.

Jason is a twenty-nine-year-old SGKA man who sought the support of RDM out of deep yearning for change. Early in our sessions, Jason stated, "I didn't have anything going for myself . . . I couldn't figure out what I was doing with my life . . . it was just a really frustrating issue . . . I just couldn't get it together . . . I knew that if I didn't go I'd be in trouble."[5] Jason heard of RDM through his ex-girlfriend, who was a member of the church where RDM is located. He initially dismissed her persistent suggestions to seek out counseling because of his assumption that only those with severe mental issues or those who were too "weak" to handle their own problems sought professional help. Jason finally decided to come in when the overwhelming pressures and expectations for his success[6] led to paralyzing feelings of regret, shame, and guilt. At RDM, he found a non-threatening place that allowed him to reflect, find understanding, and heal without risk of judgment.

Sam, a thirty-year-old SGKA heard of RDM through church announcements and brochures and directly from me, the counselor. He wanted to explore more of his identity. "The moment I realized that I wanted to know myself, but didn't know myself very well . . . I figured doing counseling would be a good way to start."[7] Sam spent most of his life focused on following and doing the things he felt he had to do, leaving him little time for discovering who he is and what brings him joy. RDM, a space to be creatively free, allowed Sam to engage in critically processing his past and the feelings, thoughts, and beliefs that led him to conclude what is true and to own it on his own terms.

Rose is a twenty-three-year-old SGKA woman who had been interested in counseling "for a while now because the [predominantly white] church I go to . . . recommend[s] people to go all the time."[8] Rose first heard about RDM through her boyfriend who attended the church where the space is located. She decided to start counseling because she was having a difficult time managing the transition from adolescence to adulthood. Her

---

5. Jason, interview by author, July 15, 2017.

6. The definition of *success* within the Korean American community is further explored in chapter 1.

7. Sam, interview by author, June 29, 2017.

8. Rose, interview by author, July 6, 2017.

many responsibilities and relationships were increasing her anxiety until the emotions felt out of control. "I felt like my heart needed something, like I needed to take care of something."[9] She chose to come to RDM because "a lot of my problems and issues come from my family and it just felt right to have someone that was Korean to counsel me because she or he would understand a little bit more."[10]

We will dive further into the lives of these four clients and their experiences at RDM in the chapters that follow. Here are some questions that emerge from these introductions: What wounded them? How have they managed their wounds and pains before coming to RDM? How do they perceive the transformations they have undergone? To what do they attribute these changes? What do they hope for themselves and for their relationships with others in the future? The following methodology assisted me in examining these questions.

Framing the Door: Methods of Research

The philosophical frameworks that inform this research are *phenomenology* and *postcolonial theory*. *Phenomenology* places value on understanding "phenomena from the actor's own perspective and describing the world as experienced by the subjects, with the assumption that the important reality is what people perceive it to be."[11] This means in this context, the client's experience and interpretation of it carry the greatest weight in a RDM counseling session. As the four clients of this study answered the interview questions (Appendix 1), I saw them make new connections and find meaning from their time in RDM. The opportunity to use their voices to share their journeys allowed for further integration and appreciation for the changes they experienced. There were several powerful and emotional moments as space was given for them to reflect on their journeys of personal growth and transformation. As they thought about and shared their experiences of this specific space, the clients could reaffirm the unshackling of their voices and their trek toward liberation and empowerment.

Postcolonial theory critiques the dominant group in how they use power. This framework is a helpful lens as it seeks to challenge the oppression of SGKAs' voices by upturning Euro-centric perspectives and creating

---

9. Rose, interview by author, July 6, 2017.
10. Rose, interview by author, July 6, 2017.
11. Kvale, *InterViews*, 30.

Introduction

room for marginal ones. Postcolonial theory identifies "the unequal and uneven forces of cultural representation, . . . the often disadvantaged, histories of nations, races, communities, [and] peoples"[12] and aims to interrupt them by highlighting the voices previously unheard. Pastoral theologian Emmanuel Lartey gives seven features of postcolonializing activities: counter-hegemonic, strategic, hybrid, interactional and intersubjective, dynamic, polyvocal, and creative.[13] This study encompasses these features as it presents the voices of those who are moving into the messiness of reforming their self-perceptions and their relations with others and the world. They are able to step into this place as they critically reflect and go against the oppressive voices that have initially placed them on the margins.

A new perspective can only happen when the oppressive forces that have pushed SGKAs to the margins are challenged and reevaluated. By examining the transformations of these four individuals as empowered human beings, this study aims to encourage a strong stance toward liberation and empowerment against oppressive forces. Although it would be irresponsible to use these voices to generalize the whole of the SGKAs' experience, this study can serve as the starting place for understanding, dialogue and progress toward justice and freedom. As mentioned earlier, the pseudonyms have been chosen by the clients themselves as they exercise their power to name who they are and how they want to be known. In chapter 2, there is further examination of the postcolonial concepts relevant to the formation of RDM and the impact this space has on the lives of its SGKA clients.

The Researcher and the Participants

As the founder and director of RDM and counselor for my four clients, I am aware of the power dynamics that are at play between the research participants and me. As researcher, I have added another role in my relationship with these four participants: I am privileged to be in the room as their counselor, witnessing their transformations. From this perspective, I am an intimate insider who has provided and continues to provide guidance for this transformation. On the other hand, I am an outsider for each clients' experience of the change that is happening within them. As I learn about their experiences during their time in RDM, I stand as an outside researcher. I noticed a shift in power and dynamics during the interview

12. Bhabha, *Location of Culture*, 245–46.
13. Lartey, *Postcolonializing God*, xvi–xviii.

as the clients teach me about their personal experiences. Even though I walked with them as a guide through these transformations, I now have become a student, gleaning information on how they experienced the phenomena of RDM in their lives.

All four clients are in their 20s to early 30s. The basis for the age range comes from research and publications of sociologist Pyong Gap Min,[14] which claim that although SGKAs and other Asian Americans face the struggle for ethnic identity and integration from childhood, it is not until college or later when they enter their professional lives that the issue comes to the foreground. Rebecca Kim's[15] and Sharon Kim's[16] works show that it is also during this age range when many SGKAs creatively form hybrid identities and third spaces. These two concepts will be unpacked further in chapter 2. This struggle for identity and integration motivates the client to come to RDM. They desire to self-explore and feel more alive.

Of the four clients I initially approached for participation, three continued in the study without any issues, and one dropped out. Soon after, a past client volunteered to participate, leaving the number of interviewees unchanged. Each client was interviewed twice, with additional opportunities for feedback and clarifications. The first set of interviews proceeded with the same set of open-ended questions; the second set of interviews stemmed from questions I had after a summary of the first set of interviews was sent to the clients for review. I also sent short excerpts from the draft of this study as it was being written when the clients' words were used to ensure my interpretation and use of their voices were accurate and not misconstrued. The following five chapters are my best attempts at a faithful and truthful rendering of the changes these clients went through in their time at RDM, their transformations, and my analysis of reoccurring themes.

---

14. Min and Kim, *Struggle for Ethnic Identity*, 11–14.

15. Rebecca Kim's *God's Whiz Kids? Korean American Evangelicals on Campus* explores how SGKAs have formed their own "emergent ethnicity" that is different from their Korean parents' generation.

16. Sharon Kim analyzes SGKA congregations in *Faith of Our Own: Second Generation Spirituality in Korean American Churches*, where young, professional SGKAs, are creating hybrid third spaces with elements of the first-generation immigrant Korean churches and elements of the mainstream evangelical American churches to create a space, uniquely their own.

Introduction

A Walk through the Red Door: Chapter Outline

Chapter 1, *Red Door Ministry in Context*, starts with the common themes of homelessness, double lives and marginality that emerge from growing up as an SGKA. The tensions and conflicts of living "in-between" two worlds—as a Korean and as an American—and not feeling at home in either is explored. This exploration is followed by examining the mental health consequences one experiences in this double life of marginalization. Next, a contextual analysis of the Korean American church gives not only a fuller picture of RDM's location but also adds to the complex picture of many SGKAs' experiences. Chapter 1 ends with the aims for RDM's conception: a place where SGKAs can move toward wholeness and find a home in themselves and in the world around them.

Chapter 2, *The Space of Red Door Ministry*, explores various definitions of space within RDM. I use the postcolonial concept of *third space,* something new—that is neither one or the other—to describe RDM as the kind of space that is formed as we engage in pastoral care and counseling in the twenty-first century, where we can no longer expect one formulaic method of counseling to be relevant for caring for people living in an increasingly intercultural world. This exploration is followed by the description of the physical space and location of RDM. Chapter 2 ends with a deep exploration of the inner space within the counselor through a personal recount of my own journey toward wholeness and finding home.

Chapter 3, *What Happens in Red Door Ministry*, takes a close look at clients' experiences as examined through the lens of shame. Western twentieth-century psychological theorists as well as Eastern theories are considered as we trace two clients move beyond shame. The clients' voices when describing their transformations are put in a dialogue with Donald W. Winnicott's concepts of transitional object, play, and true self, as well as Carl Jung's notions of self-exploration, individuation, and shadow. A critical look is taken at how these themes from Western theorists resonate in the lives of SGKAs. Eastern concepts of *jeong* and *hahn* as well as the metaphor of *fusion chef* serve as alternative frameworks that explain the clients' transformations. I conclude by examining how caregivers and the church might broaden their scope of care through education, self-critique, and immersion for responsible and relevant care in our intercultural society.

In chapter 4, *Transformations in Red Door Ministry,* I use theological reflection as a way of explaining the clients' transformations. Pulling from various pastoral theologians as well as from different social scholars,

I analyze the relationship of margins and centers. Connections are made to earlier contexts and various theories that can help us see where God may be amid this transformative process.

The last chapter, *Beyond Red Door Ministry*, imagines what going forward might look like. As individual lives change, how will clients impact their families and their communities? Although this research focuses on the experience of four SGKAs, I explore how themes raised from this study might impact the larger Korean American community, other communities of color within the United States, and the increasingly intercultural global community.

This research takes a close look at the transformations happening within RDM and gives pastoral and intercultural caregivers strategies to appropriately care for those who have too often been cast aside. RDM represents an innovative and culturally sensitive counseling model that listens to the voices of SGKAs and provide them a space for healing and empowerment. In this caregiving space, creative solutions arise that provide fresh perspectives on how to move beyond shame and places of marginality to attain wholeness, find home and create new centers.

1

Red Door Ministry in Context

There's a lot of confusion, trying to understand why . . . I'm not in a comfortable place . . . the home was very different, especially when I compared it to families who had lived in the United States much longer . . . I knew that was different, but I didn't understand why it was different . . . basically my family was going through just trying to survive . . . They didn't have a good foundation because they just moved here . . . it felt kind of lonely actually, growing up like that.[1]

—SAM, RDM CLIENT

In Search of Home

SAM EXPRESSES HIS CONFUSION, difference, displacement, and loneliness in contrast with his desire for comfort, acceptance, and home. This lack of home comes from feeling excluded, misunderstood and undervalued by the communities and mainstream society around him. Sam and many second-generation Korean Americans (SGKAs) like him long for home, understanding, and acceptance. These are necessary qualities that form a "good foundation," a home from which a whole human being develops. What happens to a person or a group of people who constantly feels

---

1. Sam, interview by author, June 29, 2017.

unwelcomed or *away* from home? What are the consequences of those who are citizens of a nation, but who are treated as perpetual foreigners? Where can they find any semblance of home, a place they feel accepted and understood? Can space be created for SGKAs to experience a homecoming, where confusion dissolves into comfort and where differences are embraced and appreciated?

Finding a home in the United States is a relatively new immigration story for Korean Americans compared to other Asian Americans such as Chinese, Japanese, or Filipino Americans. The Korean American story begins in the early twentieth century, when a few thousand Korean immigrants came to the United States as laborers for the sugar plantations in Hawaii.[2] Some of these first Korean immigrants made their way to California where they established churches,[3] showing that the relationship between Korean American churches and Korean American immigrants stems from the very beginnings of the Korean immigration to the United States. Following the Korean War in the 1950s, there was a smaller, second movement of Korean immigrants to the United States. These immigrants came as adoptees and "GI brides."[4] After the lifting of the federal immigration ban through the Immigration and Nationality Act of 1965,[5] the third and largest movement of Korean immigrants was made possible. Since this landmark legislation, the Korean American population has increased from 70,000 in 1970 to an estimated 1.7 million in 2010.[6] With this large influx of Korean immigrants entering the country in the last decades of the twentieth century, many SGKAs, those who are born in the United States or who immigrated in early childhood, are only now reaching adulthood and navigating the complexities of living in both Korean and American cultures.

Over the last decades of the twentieth century (1970s to 1990s), large enclaves of Korean Americans settled in major cities throughout the United

---

2. Fong, *Culturally Competent Practice*, 82.

3. "The Korean Methodist Church of San Francisco held its first service in October 1905 and the Korean Presbyterian Church was established in Los Angeles a year later." Kwon et al., *Korean Americans and Religions*, 9.

4. A significant number of Korean War orphans as well as orphans fathered by American soldiers were adopted by North American families. "GI" or "Government Issue," is a military slang term to refer to enlisted American soldiers. "GI Brides" are the Korean women American soldiers married when stationed in Korea during the Korean War (1950–953). Kang, *Unveiling the Self*, 46.

5. Min, *Koreans in North America*, 1.

6. Min, *Koreans in North America*, 9.

States. Among the cities and areas most populated by Korean Americans are Los Angeles, San Francisco, New York and New Jersey area, Chicago, and Washington D.C. Starting in the twenty-first century, Korean Americans began moving to cities in the southern states such as Virginia, Georgia, Florida, and Texas.[7] Red Door Ministry (RDM) is located in one of the fast-growing Korean American communities in Georgia. The Korean American population in the county where RDM is located has more than doubled from an estimated 10,000 people in the year 2000 to more than 22,500 in 2014[8] with no signs of slowing down. This demographic change also points to an increase in SGKAs, many of whom are reaching or will be reaching adulthood in the first few decades of the twenty-first century. Compared to the first generation of Korean immigrants, however, their numbers are currently relatively small. A broad demographic survey of the Korean Americans in the United States from 2014 reveals the age differentials and work patterns between the two generations:

> The mean age of second-generation single-ethnic Korean Americans is 19.5, while that of first generation Korean immigrants is 49.8. Only 25% of second-generation single-ethnic Korean Americans are at prime working ages (25–64) while 75% of first generation Korean immigrants are at their prime working ages.[9]

Based on the above figures, the number of SGKAs becoming adults and entering the workforce is likely to boom in the next couple of decades when many of the first-generation Korean immigrants enter retirement. As more SGKAs enter adulthood and join the workforce, they are becoming an important population that deserves attention and study.

Many Korean Americans living near RDM have moved from other cities in the United States for a second or third chance of attaining the American Dream.[10] What happens to this dream when United States citizens do not regard SGKAs as "fully American?" The dream can become a nightmare when SGKAs are considered "too Americanized" by first-generation Korean immigrant parents. Wedged between two worlds as not fully American or fully Korean, SGKAs may feel emotionally homeless.

---

7. Min, *Koreans in North America*, 41.

8. Yeomans, "Gwinnett Large Draw," para. 9.

9. Min and Noh, *Second-Generation Korean Experiences*, 16.

10. The Korean American version of the American Dream will be explored more in detail in the sections that follow.

Opening the Red Door

This chapter will examine the psychosocial context of SGKAs who come to RDM seeking solace from a society that does not afford them a home. The chapter first explores the double lives of SGKAs and the mental health consequences of double marginalization. The role of the Korean American church as comforter and oppressor follows. The chapter ends with introducing RDM as a place of wholeness and homecoming for SGKAs.

Double Lives

> The reality was that I lived a *double life*. At school, I was an outgoing, all-American teenager, but at home I was a good, quiet Korean girl who spoke Korean and ate Korean food. The shift from one to the other was immediate and automatic as soon as I opened the front door of my house. It was also largely unconscious.[11]
>
> —ROSE KIM, SOCIOLOGIST

> As second gens, we are almost expected to . . . cater to our first gen parents *and* to . . . American culture . . . It is interesting—the conflict that's [there] when you're trying to cater to both worlds, trying to like be successful in both areas.[12]
>
> —ROSE, RDM CLIENT

Although the shift between cultures is often unconscious, many SGKAs may feel that they do not fully fit in as persons of Korean heritage or as American citizens. In the quotes above, both Roses summarize their internal struggles. These two women are constantly pulled by two voices: the Korean one that calls for obedience and submission to parents without question and the American voice that feeds the mythology of success that advocates for their independence.

---

11. Min and Kim, *Struggle for Ethnic Identity*, 60.
12. Rose, interview by author, July 6, 2017.

Scholarship on the Double Lives of Second-Generation Korean Americans

The double life experienced by many SGKAs has been first written about by W.E.B. Du Bois in *The Soul of Black Folk* in 1903. Examining the lives of Black Americans, he describes it as "a peculiar sensation, this double-consciousness, this sense of always looking at one's self through the eyes of others."[13] SGKAs often share this sensation of "double-consciousness" as they carry both aspects of Korean and American culture within them, while simultaneously feeling like outsiders through the critical gaze of both communities. Replacing just a few descriptors, Du Bois' words ring true of the lives of many SGKAs who "feel [their] two-ness—an American, a [Korean]; two souls, two thoughts, two unreconciled strivings; two warring ideals in one . . . body, whose dogged strength alone keeps it from being torn asunder."[14] The SGKAs' struggles of living with conflicting Korean and American voices have been examined by several scholars.

Sociologist Pyong Gap Min claims that literature on the Korean American experience goes back four decades.[15] Korean American scholars, however, have focused their attention on SGKAs only in the past two decades. Most of the literature on Korean Americans before the twenty-first century has studied Korean immigrants and not their children. Min's several books on SGKAs are mainly a collection of personal narratives written by SGKAs themselves in their struggle for an ethnic identity. Min concludes that most of the SGKA contributors "experienced inner struggles over how to maintain a balance between their Korean and American identities, or how to integrate them, especially as they grew older and more aware."[16]

Examining the process of identity formation itself, Steve Kang explores the various internal voices of the SGKAs in their self-construction in *Unveiling the Sociocultural Constructed Multivoiced Self,* while David Oh looks at the role of transnational media such as the rise in global popularity of K-pop, Korean dramas, and movies in *Second-Generation Korean Americans and Transnational Media.* Dae Young Kim writes about the double marginalization many SGKAs feel in *Second-Generation Korean Americans: The Struggle for Full Inclusion.* Grace Yoo and Barbara Kim add another

---

13. Du Bois, *Souls of Black Folk,* 8.
14. Du Bois, *Souls of Black Folk,* 8.
15. Min, "Four-Decade Literature," 195–252.
16. Park et al., *Younger-Generation Korean Experiences,* 225.

layer of complexity as they look at the mix of obligation and desire SGKAs have in caring for and fulfilling their aging parents' expectation in *Caring Across Generations*. Most of these authors mention the critical role of faith and the Korean American church in the SGKAs' struggle with identity and living a double life.

Framing the SGKAs experience through a religious perspective, both Rebecca Kim in *God's Whiz Kid* and Sharon Kim in *A Faith of Our Own* study the emerging hybrid identity SGKAs are starting to embrace in places of worship. Mark Hearn in *Religious Experience Among Second Generation Korean Americans*, Christine Hong in *Identity, Youth, and Gender in the Korean American Church*, and Jacob Young in *Korean, Asian, or American?* use the Korean American church as the base of studying the SGKAs experience of gender, spirituality, and ethnic identity. The themes of living a double life, feeling misunderstood or unaccepted, and struggling to feel at home are repeated in the creation of an Asian American theology by four Korean American theologians.

Andrew Park lays out the marginal existence and possible theological implications of living as Korean Americans in *Racial Conflict and Healing: An Asian-American Theological Perspective*. *From a Liminal Place: an Asian American Theology*, by Sang Hyun Lee, stretches the notion of marginality by claiming the benefits and value of being in a liminal place. Similarly, Joseph Cheah and Grace Ji-Sun Kim's *Theological Reflections on "Gangnam Style"* challenges SGKAs and other Korean Americans to see their location in the margins of society as the place for prophetic vision and voice. These theological explorations give room for the analysis of the struggle and sufferings of living a double life, but also encourages the possible positives of living in two worlds. They also claim this double life as divinely appointed to add value and meaning not just to the Korean American community, but also to mainstream American society.

The Benefits of a Double Life

Being bicultural has many benefits. SGKAs' can contribute to their Korean American community as well as to the larger society of the United States. The ability of SGKAs to flow in and out of both cultures places them in a unique position as bridges between Korean and American culture, allowing people on both sides to expand their horizons and help one another.[17]

17. For example, "second-generation leaders were able to use personal contacts at

The high cultural pressures to succeed have led many SGKAs to attain higher education levels. According to the American Community Survey from 2010, "72.3% of U.S.-born Koreans between 23 and 35, compared to 35.5% of whites, graduated from college."[18] Despite these positives, living in two different worlds comes with an intense sense of marginality. The negative psychological and emotional effect of being bicultural and living a double life varies for each SGKAs, but there are multiple commonalities. The internal conflict and tensions many SGKAs feel are often heightened by the struggle for full inclusion in the Korean American community and mainstream American society as well as from the pressures to succeed from both sides.

Not Fully Korean

A Snapshot of Korean Culture

Heavily influenced by centuries of Confucian ideology, traditional Koreans see the family as the most accessible unit for living out the proper relationships that will lead to a harmonious community and a prosperous nation. "The most important relationship of all for Confucius is the one between a son and his father."[19] In the parent-child relationship, filial piety is the accepted virtue, which is interpreted by many as obedience without question and submission without rebellion. This ensures harmony within the home, which is believed to ripple out to support a benevolent and strong society.

Like many other Eastern cultures, Koreans also place emphasis on the collective good over the Western notion of the individual. Feelings, thoughts, and behaviors are construed with the larger group in mind. In Korean culture, "a person's action and life are not just his or her own, but they both represent and reflect his or her extended family and ancestors . . . Obligation and shame, are used to maintain sociocultural norms and expectations."[20] Selfhood and one's identity is defined in terms of relation-

---

their companies to bring many representatives of American corporations to the [Korean American Community Foundation] gala . . . rais[ing] a fund of approximately one million dollars . . . to fund Korean social service organizations." Min, *Koreans in North America*, 71.

18. Kim, *Second-Generation Korean Americans*, 21.
19. Stevenson et al., *Twelve Theories of Human Nature*, 25.
20. Kang, *Unveiling the Self*, 94.

ships rather than one's own being. This contrasting view of the self creates tension between the first and second generations.

Korean Culture vs. American[21] Culture

Many Korean immigrant parents hold firmly to this traditional view of family and the collective good while their children grow up in the United States where they are taught Western values of reason, criticism, and individualism. Psychologist Rowena Fong claims, "immigrant[s] . . . in new environments may cling to their cultural values with a fresh intensity in reaction to the fear of losing the old culture in the new environment."[22] Korean immigrants' cultural ties to their homelands provide the stability they need while they adjust in a foreign land. For most SGKAs, this retention of traditional Korean family ties creates tension and conflict within them as they straddle different worlds. Outside the home, SGKAs are taught the importance of speaking and expressing their thoughts and emotions, which directly contradicts the expectations of quiet submission and placing the family's needs above one's own at home.[23] In a traditional Korean household, sharing one's opinions and feelings that differ from the older generation is seen as a sign of deep disrespect and is rarely tolerated. For many SGKAs, speaking up, which is encouraged in school, is quickly silenced and even punished at home. This creates a family environment that is volatile because of intergenerational stress and tension.

Young Lee Hertig complicates the issue by saying, "To an already challenging family life, cross-cultural migration adds further difficulties as each family member acculturates at a different pace."[24] As children quickly adapt to Western attitudes and values, many parents are culturally stuck in their home country's value system as it was when they immigrated, even as their home country's culture continues to change. It is as if they are living in a home culture that is frozen in time. The second-generation children

---

21. With apologies to those in Canada and Latin America, the term "American" will be used in this chapter to refer to the mainstream culture and dominant groups of the United States of America.

22. Fong, *Culturally Competent Practice*, 7.

23. "In traditional Korean family, filial piety, family ties and obedience to one's own parents always takes precedence over one's own personal needs." Son, *Motives of Self-Sacrifice*, 14.

24. Hertig, *Cultural Tug of War*, 16.

of these immigrants are often raised in the older Korean value system of strict gender roles and Confucian norms that not only are disconnected from American culture but are also considered outdated in contemporary Korean culture as well.

Exposed to American culture and media where expressions of parental love and affections are abundant, SGKAs long for external affirmations of love and encouragements from their parents. Many Korean immigrant parents, however, "do not openly praise their children because they feel that this could inflate their ego . . . As such, [SGKAs] might interpret their parents' behavior as a sign of disapproval or a lack of parental love and acceptance."[25] Confucian values of maintaining rigid hierarchies and social order within the home also creates emotional distance between parent and child for the sake of proper harmonious relationships. Steve Kang explains, "Korean American fathers were especially socialized to keep a distance from their children and not to express much affection to them. Influenced by Confucian teachings, many believe that intimacy with children undermines the children's respect for their parents."[26] These layers of differences add to the frustrations and misunderstandings that can create large gaps between parents and children.

"Too Americanized"

SGKAs are marginalized by the first-generation Korean Americans because they are seen as "too Americanized" to be fully accepted as Koreans. Although the degree of language fluency varies, SGKAs are generally able to understand Korean better than they can use it. Many SGKAs grasp enough of the Korean language to understand the criticism of their parents' generation that they are *too* Americanized. Korean/Korean American culture, however, denies SGKAs the power to respond on equal grounds to the older generation due to their youth. This response is further encumbered by their lack of fluency in Korean.

Due to generational power differentials, many adult SGKAs' voices are not given the same weight or value as the first-generation Korean Americans within the Korean American community. This phenomenon is noticeable in the context of some Korean American churches which I explore later in this chapter. For the first-generation Korean parents, their

25. Rhee "Impact of Immigration," 108.
26. Kang, *Unveiling the Self*, 119–20.

children and other SGKAs are Americans who grew up without the cultural experience or knowledge of being Korean. Although they may physically look Korean, many first-generation Korean Americans see SGKAs as culturally Americans.

Not Fully American

The Myth

The myth that the United States is a land of equality, freedom, and opportunity for all stems from the very beginning of its formation through the immortalized words found in the Declaration of Independence. Thomas Jefferson optimistically writes,

> We hold these truths to be self-evident, that all men [sic] are created equal, that they are endowed by their Creator with certain unalienable Rights, that among these are Life, Liberty and the pursuit of Happiness.[27]

People throughout the world have immigrated to the United States in pursuit of their own life, liberty, and the pursuit of happiness. History, however, depicts how race has been the dividing line that excludes non-whites from full citizenship.[28] It was not until the second half of the twentieth century with the Civil Rights Act of 1964, the Voting Rights Act, and the Immigration Act of 1965 that a more egalitarian version of the country seemed to be achievable, at least on paper.[29] Much of the experience of non-white Americans, however, continues to be one of marginalization and inequality.

Being "Asian American"

SGKAs, like other Korean Americans and Asian Americans, are marginalized by American society. They are seen by many Americans as part of the larger Asian American group. It must be said that although there may be some similarities shared among Asian American cultures, such as the

---

27. Jefferson, "Declaration of Independence," para. 2.

28. Non-white citizens were denied the right to vote, or denied citizenship itself despite being born in the United Sates, as in the case of many Asians and Middle Easterners, well into the twentieth century. Spickard, *Almost All Aliens*, 227–340.

29. Spickard, *Almost All Aliens*, 337.

influence of Confucianism, vast differences exist within each Asian American subgroup. Many Asian Americans, with the exception of political and academic circles, rarely identify themselves as Asian American, but rather more identify with their ethnic groups. Similar marginal treatment from American society, however, allows for common experiences that many Asian Americans share, forming a connection with one another, despite their different ethnicities and nationalities. The term "Asian" itself is political and is a colonial response to the powers of the West giving it anti-European roots. In the United States, the term "Asian" is used to lump together diverse, different nationalities as one, making it easier for mainstream American society to digest and relate to a group of peoples who are racially different. The term is also necessary as Asian Americans band together to continue their "political struggle and resistance against racism."[30] Although not all SGKAs identify as Asian Americans, I will use this label for the purposes of understanding SGKAs' experiences of being perceived as Asians in the United States based on their physical appearance. With this in mind, the term "Asian American" will be used interchangeably with SGKA when appropriate in this context.

Racism Intensified

SGKAs report much higher racial discrimination than the first-generation Korean Americans.[31] This perceived difference is most likely because SGKAs have heightened awareness of the subtler forms of racism that they face regularly. SGKAs are often asked questions, such as "Where are you from?"[32] or "Do you know how to speak English?"[33] that show racial stereotyping and prejudice. Interpersonal racism is often first experienced from an early age at school. Their external Asian appearance leads to racist comments and even violence because many SGKAs are bullied in school.[34] Jason shares, "growing up [in school] there was the whole 'ching, chang chong,' 'chink' . . . I've been in so many fights over stupid racist comments . . . even me too, I would say stuff, I wasn't actually racist, but I would say those things . . . to

---

30. Kim, "The 'Indigestible' Asian," 37.
31. Young, *Korean, Asian, or American*, 17.
32. Kim, *Second-Generation Korean Americans*, 103.
33. Kim, *Second-Generation Korean Americans*, 98.
34. Tseng et al., "Asia Americans' Education Experiences," 117.

get back at them."³⁵ For SGKAs for whom the United States is the only home they know, the racism they experience feels painful and confusing.

> Given that racial othering reoccurs and accumulates over time, these encounters remind second-generation Koreans of their racial and cultural differences and the intractability of race. Not only do these exchanges stigmatize their self-identities, often leaving lasting impressions on their psyches, but also they remind them of the contingent and elusive condition of inclusion into the mainstream.³⁶

The sense of unwelcome experienced by SGKAs in the United States goes beyond racist comments as mainstream American society refuse to see them as legitimate American citizens.

Forever Foreigners

Little room remains in the collective American consciousness for Korean Americans or other Asian Americans to be part of what makes up American citizenship. Ava shares an encounter she had as a nurse in the labor and delivery unit as an example:

> Ava: I feel like [white Americans] don't understand that [Asian] Americans can still be American . . . this one instance at work where an Indian family was . . . [asking] the white nurse to pronounce the name [of their newborn baby] . . . she was totally oblivious, ignorant . . . So the family asked and she said it correctly and . . . the parents were like, "oh you said it correctly, that is how you pronounce it." and she was like "yeah, I have a lot of families ask just to make sure *Americans* can pronounce it correctly." She said that like three times, three different ways, like *Americans* can pronounce it, to see if *Americans* can . . . and I'm like "oh my gosh!"
>
> Author/Interviewer: as if *they* are not Americans?
>
> Ava: Yeah! I'm like, "How do you know if they're not Americans." They're speaking in English like, perfectly fine. It just irked me, every time she said it . . . I don't think they know that we are Americans, honestly!³⁷

---

35. Jason, interview by author, July 15, 2017.
36. Kim, *Second-Generation Korean Americans*, 97.
37. Ava, interview by author, July 5, 2017.

Ava is talking about a common experience shared by many Asian Americans, having a feeling of being a "perpetual foreigner." Regardless of having been born in the United States, Korean Americans, like other Asian Americans, are seen as "forever foreigners" in the eyes of far too many in America because of their race.

Mia Tuan, a fellow second generation Asian American, captures Ava's sentiment: "What it means to be an American continues to demand European ancestry. Whites continue to feel a sense of 'proprietary claim' to being the 'real' American."[38] This sentiment has gained more momentum under Donald Trump's presidency. Ava continues, "after he became president I feel like everything has just heightened . . . I feel like people are more aware that they're a minority or more aware that they are 'different' after he became president . . . like we are unwelcomed."[39] For SGKAs, there is a sense that all non-white, "perpetual foreigners" are under the gaze of "real" Americans, as violent encounters based on race become more frequent throughout the country. Ava talks about an event that led to a heightened awareness of her race:

> There was this one *halmuni* (Korean grandmother) walking down the street who literally just got punched in the face . . . she literally got knocked out by this white woman who like ran off . . . I knew people thought like that . . . We're appearance-wise . . . different and on top of that, seeing the news, I'm more alert or sensitive that people are staring.[40]

This feeling of unwelcome and being treated as a forever foreigner have been exacerbated by the Covid-19 pandemic. With the virus originating from China, Asian Americans have reported over 3,800 documented anti-Asian hate incidents[41] since March of 2020 when the pandemic reached the United States. This number continues to grow daily as Asian Americans experience increased anxiety over "being targeted after President Donald Trump used racist language to describe the coronavirus. Critics warned his repeated use of phrases like 'Chinese virus' and 'kung flu' could escalate attacks on Asian Americans." [42] Weaker members of the Asian American population, such as school children and seniors, have often been the target

---

38. Tuan, "Second Generation Identity," 235.
39. Ava, interview by author, July 5, 2017.
40. Ava, interview by author, July 5, 2017.
41. Smith, "Anti-Asian Hate Crimes," para. 13.
42. Balingt et al., "As school reopen," para. 11.

of these hate crimes, some of which have ended in death.[43] SGKAs are outraged and hurt by this painful reminder that as Asian Americans, they are rejected and marginalized by their fellow citizens. Many are organizing together to speak out against this racially motivated violence and aggression by other American citizens.

Denied full inclusion in the Korean American community as well as the mainstream American society, many SGKAs feel like strangers unwelcomed in both contexts. This exclusion nurtures feelings of loneliness and of being misunderstood, which are further heightened by the pressures from both sides to fit in.

Pressures to Fit In

Expectations from Korean American Parents

SGKA's desire to find a home where they are accepted and understood is further complicated by the high expectations of their parents. One such expectation is for them to act as cultural liaisons. With their lack of English proficiency, many first-generation Korean Americans depend on their children to act as translators, ranging from mundane activities such as managing bills to large decisions such as securing a mortgage. "Children help with their family's economic survival, and roles reverse as these children—at young ages—navigate culture, language, and racism for their immigrant parents and care for their economic survival."[44] This common experience of acting as translators often has negative consequences for SGKAs because many report having "a low level of respect for their parents and were often embarrassed by [their parents] in public settings."[45] Thrust into these adult roles, young SGKAs are often robbed of their childhood as they are placed in the foreground of managing their family's finances. Not only do many lose respect for their parents, but they also vacillate between feeling frustrated at their parents for their lack of competence and feeling guilty for not being a "good" child who willingly helps the family. Ava, a client from RDM, explains this internal conflict:

---

43. On March 16, 2021, eight people were shot in several massage parlors by the same white man, six of whom were Asian American women, four of whom were Korean Americans. Many believe these incidents were racially motivated. Fausset and Vigdor, "8 People Killed in Atlanta," para. 1–22.

44. Yoo, *Caring across Generations*, 15.

45. Kim, *Faith of Our Own*, 62.

> I think that's something nobody understands unless you are second generation—having to translate ... I get really frustrated with her, like, shikyu-ing [delegating] stuff to me, ... there's been a handful of times when I just would not be in mood to translate something for her and call somewhere. That would spark my mom to be very emotional and cry ... and be like "you know if I knew how to speak English then I would do this, wae nuh hantae shikyu? (why would I make you do it?) if I were able to" and of course that would make me feel—"oh, crap, fine! ok."[46]

Ava struggles with wanting to be a good daughter by helping her mom, while also trying to focus on the demands of her own life. This expectation has caused not only a bigger disconnect between parent and child, but has also demanded much of the energy and time SGKAs could be using for their own identity and emotional development.

Although being cultural brokers for their parents adds unnecessary stress for the SGKAs, the enormous pressures the parents place on their children's academic and financial success outweighs any other expectations, becoming one of the biggest stressors for this population. The Korean American community has a set formula that equates educational achievement with the guaranteed road for financial success. In turn, financial stability is the tangible expression of having successfully arrived in America.

Korean American Dream

A Korean American version of the American Dream is often defined by "financial success, develop[ment of] self [by] attaining as much education as possible ... and achiev[ing] an autonomous life."[47] Most SGKAs grow up hearing:

> the strong and consistent message that they are the reason why their parents immigrated to the United States, and observed the losses and hardships that came with immigration as their parent sought to achieve their "Korean American dream" of stability and establishment.[48]

In practical terms, the Korean American Dream includes having a desirable house in the suburbs, attending elite schools, pursuing a professional

---

46. Ava, interview by author, July 5, 2017.
47. Kang, *Unveiling the Self*, 163–64.
48. Yoo, *Caring across Generations*, 68.

career,[49] and marrying a Korean American partner.[50] This narrow definition of success is further reinforced by "Korean language newspapers and radio and television stations . . . [that] actively provide . . . news stories of Korean high school valedictorians as well as reports of school rankings and school districts and success stories of famous Korean Americans."[51]

Although Korean immigrants came from various socioeconomic backgrounds, many first-generation Korean Americans have found themselves being underpaid or underemployed due to their lack of proficiency in the English language, as well as the blatant racism they encountered upon arrival. Rather than suffer under such circumstances, many first-generation Korean Americans have opted to start small businesses or work for other Korean Americans.[52] With rarely any days of rest, a large majority of first-generation Korean Americans often work long hours, six to seven days a week, as private business owners or as employees of Korean-owned small businesses. SGKAs see the hardships and sacrifices their parents have made for them and take it upon themselves to be the successful result of their parent's hard work. Rose talks about having this strong feeling that "I . . . owe something to them . . . they've given their lives to me! (Sigh) and they've worked for whatever years of their lives in harsh conditions . . . and I'm like, 'umm, I didn't choose this life for you.'"[53] SGKAs are expected to make the most of educational opportunities and be financially successful as the fruits of their parents' choices and sacrifice. Like Rose, many SGKAs feel stuck fulfilling this expectation for the choices their parents made. She continues to explain that she was not given a choice in pursuing her own career path.

> It's not necessarily that they want us to get good grades, it's that they want us to like, be successful and not have to worry about money and like I can guarantee you that because my mom did not know what a nurse does, like because she didn't like, fully understand how much money a nurse receives, how they are treated, what kind of hours they have, that kind of stuff, she couldn't have underst[ood]. She wanted me to be a pharmacist all my life and I never did it. But it was because she knew it was a stable job and she

---

49. Kim, *Second-Generation Korean Americans*, 35.

50. "Marrying right often means choosing a partner who is Korean, and (at least) college-educated; Korean Christian parent may equally emphasize religious background." Yoo, *Caring across Generations*, 57.

51. Kim, *Second-Generation Korean Americans*, 36.

52. Min. *Koreans in North America*, 57.

53. Rose, interview by author, July 6, 2017

knew that pharmacists received a lot of money and like the hours are not that bad, etc[54]

Once her mother realized that being a nurse met the financial standards she had placed on Rose, she has stopped pressing Rose to become a pharmacist and accepted Rose's chosen career path.

For Korean immigrant parents such as Rose's, more is at stake in these expectations than simply a better financial future for themselves and their children. Many parents seek to find their lost sense of dignity and worth from the painful experience of immigration through their children. With so much of their own worth stemming from the academic performance and financial success of their children,[55] a SGKA's success or failure becomes their parent's success or failure. This situation leads to a highly competitive atmosphere within the Korean American community as first-generation Korean American parents try to stack up their children's achievements against other SGKAs with their own self-worth and self-esteem at stake. SGKAs then internalize their parents' constant comparing of them with others, making it easy for the SGKAs to start comparing themselves to others within their SGKA peer group. This in turn leads to the SGKAs to have their own struggles with self-esteem and self-worth.

Expectations from American Society

One might think that there is refuge for the SGKA outside of their community, but the expectations of being studious and financially successful follow SGKAs due to the ubiquity of the "model minority" image for Asian Americans. Because many white Americans lump SGKAs as part of the larger Asian American community, the widespread image of the "model minority" adds societal pressure to the SGKAs. Coined by sociologist William Petersen in his 1966 article about the success of the Japanese and Chinese Americans, the term "model minority" has been extended to be used for all Asian Americans.[56] This stereotype of "model minority" asserts that "Asian Americans have achieved enormous economic and academic

---

54. Rose, interview by author, July 6, 2017.

55. "The emphasis on educational success is directed not only to the student but also to the parent . . . a good parent is one whose children do well in school." Okagaki and Bojczyk, "Perspectives on Development," 85.

56. Maddux, "Model Minority," 74.

success by working hard and following Asian cultural norms."[57] Although seemingly complimentary of Asian work ethics and cultural norms, Asian Americans are therefore, as representatives of their group, expected to be more studious and to work more diligently than those in other groups. This stereotype has various downsides. Because Asian Americans are expected to succeed, their achievements are rarely celebrated; and there is even less room for "failure." Another negative implication is how Asians are used as a comparison to other non-white Americans:

> An implication of the model minority myth is that structural and systemic racism, if it exists, is not an insurmountable barrier . . . in other words, if you remain silent rather than making political waves, and work hard rather than relying on welfare, you will overcome sociopolitical obstacles and attain upward mobility in American society. [58]

This model minority myth has been used by some white Americans to blame other non-white populations, such as the Black and Latinx communities, for their lack of upward mobility. Rather than taking responsibility for and reformulating the discriminatory systems and structures of the American society they have created, the image of model minority excuses white Americans from the willingness to do the hard work required to dismantle these structures. Asian Americans have been used as an example of the possibility of achieving the American Dream, a façade that hides the great divide of class and race in this country. SGKAs are exposed to this image early on and some feel they must act in ways that are consistent with these "model minority" expectations, which reinforces the pressures for success that their parents place on them at home.

With a lack of acceptance from the Korean American community as well as from mainstream American society, SGKAs live lives of double marginalization. The pressures to succeed from both sides intensify their feelings of homelessness, rejection, and fragmentation. "They find no real place to call their home. They are straddling two places and really have nowhere to go."[59] Such divisiveness leaves SGKAs with few places of acceptance where they can be valued as whole human beings. In search of wholeness, SGKAs may find their mental health at risk.

---

57. Alvarez, *Asian American Psychology*, 70.
58. Cheah and Kim, *Reflections on "Gangnam Style,"* 17.
59. Kim, *Holy Spirit, Chi*, 88.

Mental Health Consequences of Double Lives

On the sidelines of American consciousness and on the margins of the Korean American community, SGKAs face painful disadvantages in the formation of a healthy sense of self. For many SGKAs, both American society and the Korean American community deny them full membership. This predicament of being in both, while not fully allowed to participate in either, can lead to a fragmented identity as well as a highly self-critical attitude. Feeling inadequate to be accepted by either culture, many SGKAs feel shame, low self-esteem, and a high degree of inner tension. Studies have shown that SGKA's experience higher rates of depression and anxiety in comparison to their European American counterparts and even among other Asian American populations, such as Chinese Americans, Filipino Americans, and Japanese Americans.[60] An early study of Korean American college students in 1987 correlated the higher rates of depression with struggles with "parental traditionalism."[61] This may be because Korean Americans are more recent immigrants who maintain and expect closer following of their traditional cultures than other Asian American groups.

Anger and Violence

Fatherlessness: Growing Up with Violence

With the Confucian belief that an external display of paternal affection and intimacy would lessen respect from their children, many Korean immigrant men refrain from positive expression of their emotions. In fact, most SGKAs report "having minimal interactions with their fathers . . . they also perceive that their fathers were emotionally detached from the family much of the time, with an exception of occasional angry outbursts."[62] Anger and violence are often the only emotions many SGKAs have seen from their fathers. One SGKA summarizes his interactions with his father: "[he] abused me, [he] beat me. It was very difficult, but I think it was because that's the only way [he] knew how to raise [his] kids."[63] Many SGKAs have grown up fearful of their fathers whose anger and violence acted as the emotional

---

60. Rhee, "Impact of immigration," 90.
61. Wong, "Depression Level," 51.
62. Kang, *Unveiling the Self*, 142.
63. Yoo, *Caring across Generations*, 35.

release valve for the "stressful situations within and outside the home, such as financial problems, problems at the workplace, discrimination and language barriers"[64] that immigrant life entails.

These constant stressors leave many Korean immigrant men feeling vulnerable and helpless as their self-worth and self-esteem are challenged. The economic necessity for their wives to work outside the home and become "more Americanized and assertive"[65] increases this perceived threat to their ego. The emotional wounds of racism, poverty, and acculturation as well as the breakdown of traditional patriarchal structures at home cause many first-generation Korean American men to resort to violence to reclaim their power and manhood. For example, a mental health survey from 1996 shows that, "sixty percent of a sample of immigrant Korean women in Chicago reported having been physically abused [by Korean men]. This abuse was most frequent and severe during the initial years following immigration."[66] Practical theologian Mark Hearn describes a study from 2007, which found that irrespective of generation, 79% of Korean American men had perpetuated some form of spousal abuse.[67] One must assume these to be conservative numbers given the Korean American culture of shame and "loss of face" that would preclude some victims from reporting abuse.

Anger and Violence and Second-Generation Korean Americans

SGKA men who see anger and violence as acceptable ways of expressing negative emotions have internalized a dangerous pathway to regain power and control when they feel weak or unmanly. Their aggression and oppression of women within their own group may be rooted in several factors such as loss of social status or the feminization of Asian men by the American public. Many SGKA men have been raised with the traditional values of men exerting their power at home through aggression and oppression of women. In mainstream American society, however, Asian American men are missing in positions of management and underrepresented politically[68] due to underlying institutional racism. Asian men are most visible to the American public through the media, such as television shows and Hollywood movies,

64. Yoo, *Caring across Generations*, 34.
65. Kang, *Unveiling the Self*, 115.
66. Hall, "Culture-Specific Violence," 161.
67. Hearn, *Religious Experience*, 56.
68. Hearn, *Religious Experience*, 28–34.

where they are often represented as nonthreatening jesters, as martial artists with no sex appeal or as a socially awkward nerd.[69] Asian American men rarely have lead roles in movies or television and are "often relegated to roles as tech nerds, assistants, doctors, [and] sometimes [as] highly emasculated, desexualized characters."[70] These damaging stereotypes that have deep historically racist roots continue to be perpetuated, adding to the feeling of powerlessness SGKA men may feel in American society, which exacerbates their depression and fragmentation. Unfortunately, "many of these men . . . are drawn to physical violence as a way to demonstrate their power and attain some measure of control and authority."[71]

By having a lack of development in their self-worth and a mistaken view of vulnerability as weakness, SKGA men who see anger and violence as acceptable may turn to the familiar patterns that they have witnessed at home to work through these issues. This behavior results in many SGKA women who become victims of battery or emotional trauma at home and rape by their acquaintances or men in authority. The shame resultant from such encounters means SGKAs are reluctant to speak about these experiences.

I use my own story of rape and emotional trauma from violence to connect with countless SGKA women and men who enter through RDM. Sharing my own story has opened the door for other SGKAs to tell their own experiences of anger and violence. This unspoken commonality of violence and trauma in the SGKAs' experience must no longer be kept silent. SGKA men and women must be given the space and tools to work out their injuries in healthier ways.

Quest for Success: Guilt, Shame and Fear of Failure

The intense pressure to achieve the Korean American Dream and to live up to the image of the "model minority" also creates great mental and emotional distress for SGKAs. They are flooded with feelings of shame and guilt when they feel they are unable to meet these expectations. Jacob Young, a Korean American practical theologian, explains: "guilt is often used by the parents to remind their children of the sacrifice which the parents made for the upward mobility of their children."[72] Feeling that he had failed to

69. Cheah and Kim, *Reflections on "Gangnam Style,"* 14–23.
70. Levin, "We're the Geeks," para. 4
71. Hearn, *Religious Experience*, 103.
72. Young, *Korean, Asian, or American*, 43.

meet these high expectations, Jason came to RDM with deep feelings of shame and guilt. "I had the weight of the world on my shoulders . . . I had my family waiting on my success . . . my mom waiting for me to take care of her after she'd basically given her life up to give me the opportunities that I had."[73] Jason had just dropped out of graduate school because he could not continue on a path in which he had no interest. The internal conflict of choosing what he wanted versus what was expected of him was suffocating him. Jason understood this guilt to not only be a personal one, but to also be a common struggle many SGKAs experience.

> Most parents came from Korea and they had it hard and that creates a lot of guilt too, like they worked so hard to provide you with this opportunity and if you don't take advantage of this opportunity to the fullest then you're a failure . . . then they compare you to the people who did do it the "right" way, etc . . . a lot of second gen, well for me, you know we grew up poor and I'm sure that a lot of people did that too . . . that was tough. [74]

Growing up in a home that struggled financially causes many children of immigrants to feel more pressure to succeed and to take care of their parents.

Defining success in such narrow economic terms leads to feelings of guilt, shame, and fear of failure, and creates large emotional and communication barriers between parent and child, adding to a sense of isolation and disconnection. The fear of disappointing their parents have led some SGKAs "to not only lie to parents about grades, but also resort to cheating, cutting classes, cramming, and doing the minimum to pass classes. Furthermore, an increase in suicides and mental health problems has accompanied these pressures for educational success."[75] Many SGKAs who feel they have not met this definition of success, made blatantly clear by the constant comparisons to their peers, suffer from low self-esteem and have feelings of worthlessness and "issues of inner defectives and destructiveness towards themselves."[76]

---

73. Jason, interview by author, July 15, 2017.
74. Jason, interview by author, July 15, 2017.
75. Kim, *Second-Generation Korean Americans*, 45.
76. Kang, *Unveiling the Self*, 157.

Red Door Ministry in Context

A New Definition of Success

SGKAs who *have* fulfilled the expectations of parents and society in school and work, also struggle to find the joy and wholeness they had hoped would follow their success. Researchers Nadia Kim and Christine Oh write:

> Korean-American students mostly defined "success" not as elite school admissions or high-paying careers, but as being "happy." They define success in this manner as they can identify SGKAs who are "good students, like them, [but are] clearly not happy."[77]

Unlike their parents who may define success as economic mobility, many SGKAs measure success by their emotional well-being. Sam explains, "for my parents the fact I got into [a prestigious university] and had good grades and had a job right after school... that's all they would talk about in front of their friends... [but] it's not about the success, the appearances... those are not the things that bring me joy."[78] Even with financial stability, Sam is looking for the "success" that comes from joy and inner peace. With different perspectives on success, and the high expectations and minimal emotional support from their parents, it is not surprising that many SGKAs often feel misunderstood and their emotions undervalued. The most common theme with which clients of RDM struggle is feeling inadequate, unlovable, or unacceptable unless they have *perfect* performance. Ironically, the rejection SGKAs feel from both American society and their Korean immigrant parents makes their attempts at achieving perfection only more difficult. Many SGKAs may need help in facing these struggles, but could feel hesitant in reaching out for fear of appearing weak or being stigmatized as a failure.

A Sign of Weakness: Shame

It is clear SGKAs would benefit from counseling. In the Asian American community, however, a stigma against counseling persists. As a result, many SGKAs do not seek professional care.

> Despite the evidence of high rates of mental health problems... Asians are far less likely to utilize mental health services, as compared with other ethnic/racial group members... those who manage to come to the attention of mental health professionals tend to

---

77. Kim and Oh. "A Successful Failure," 180.
78. Sam, interview by author, June 29, 2017.

exhibit more severe and chronic symptoms in comparison with non-Asians. Thus, evidence indicates that Asian Americans, when they use formal mental health care, tend to initiate treatment much later and terminate treatment more prematurely.[79]

Coming from a culture of shame and the importance of not losing face, going to see any mental health professional may be seen as a weakness, failure, or inferiority. Speaking candidly about unpleasant family matters to an outsider is also frowned upon and seen as dishonoring one's family. Counseling goes against the cultural emphasis of presenting your "best face forward" because honest and critical reexamination of self and one's relationships are needed for any real work to occur. Although some evidence exists of SGKAs' growing openness to utilize psychotherapy[80] and other mental health services, most Korean Americans from both generations have turned to religion and the church for emotional release and healing.

The Double Life of The Korean American Church

The Church as a Comforter

As a Buffer from Oppression: Marginality and Racism

The Korean American church serves not only as the religious center for spiritual nourishment but also as a cultural institution that meets a large portion of the Korean Americans' social, psychological, and emotional needs. The church has become one of the few places where Korean Americans feel welcomed and valued as dignified human beings. It is estimated 70% of all Korean Americans are members of a protestant Korean American church.[81]

For some SGKAs, their religious identity has superseded their ethnic identity because they find solace in their identification as children of God, created in God's image. Young explains: "They do this in order to overcome their inferior feelings in society and enhance self-esteem through the

---

79. Rhee, "Impact of Immigration," 90.

80. "Our sample of children of Korean immigrants, especially women, seems to be open to using psychotherapy to resolve familial and personal issues and to benefit from seeking such services." Yoo, *Caring across Generations*, 67.

81. Warner, "Korean Immigrant Church," 30.

theological proclamation that all children of God are equal."[82] Much of the pains of marginality Korean Americans experience both at home and in society is countered in this theological understanding of human beings. The unconditional love of God must also offer an attractive message for SGKAs who feel they must earn love from their parents and earn their place in mainstream American society. Thus, the concepts of unconditional love and *imago dei* give SGKAs a new perspective of self as well as alternate ways of coping with their marginal existence through prayer and fellowship:

> The church has primarily functioned as a safe haven for the young people to gather together with their cohorts. They considered the church as a place where they did not have to constantly explain their ethnic and cultural backgrounds . . . just being with fellow Korean Americans validated their identity.[83]

Coming together with other SGKAs and other second-generation Asian Americans helps SGKAs escape some of the feelings of marginality and racism. The fellowship and community they form within the church create a sense of belonging SGKAs rarely find. Some SGKA congregations are forming a distinctive hybrid identification that affirms the cultural and spiritual influences of both worlds of which they are part.[84] Unfortunately, the messages of love and acceptance do not always line up with the lived experience SGKAs have within the Korean American church.

The Church as an Oppressor

Social Hierarchy: Competition

Like the internal distress felt by many SKGAs and the intergenerational conflicts seen within the home, the church is a system that exhibits similar tensions and conflicts on a larger scale. Although the benefits of the frequent gathering of SGKAs at church are discussed above, a negative effect also arises from the comparisons they may make with their peers. Brenda Chung, a SGKA writes about her experience:

> I encountered more prejudice from other Korean kids than I did from white American kids . . . being the immigrant children of

---

82. Young, *Korean, Asian, or American*, 60.
83. Kang, *Unveiling the Self*, 199.
84. Kim, *Faith of Our Own*, 3.

a homogeneous people who have a hierarchical social structure meant that there was an expectation of conformity . . . Making good grades in school, what type of business someone's family ran, or even what kind of car someone's parents drove . . . This level of scrutiny resulted in a feeling of competiveness. And in conforming to what would become the Korean-American ideal[85]

Rather than being a place of acceptance, the church can add to the pressures of being SGKA with the need to conform to "the Korean-American ideal" by achieving the Korean American Dream. In such comparisons, most SGKAs feel that they are on the losing side of their group. Feeling judged and rejected by their own people can feel more painful than being rejected by people of different groups. Jason experienced the pressures and expectations from constant comparisons with other SGKAs: "People don't feel like they're good enough or they're not as good as their peers and that's how I felt my whole life, I always got compared to my cousin, and other [SGKA] people from church."[86] Jason started to internalize these comparisons and they fueled his feelings of shame, guilt, and anxiety. This feeling of rejection is also acutely felt in intergenerational relationships with the first generation.

Generational Hierarchy

As mentioned earlier, many first-generation Korean Americans do not accept SGKAs as full Koreans. This lack of acceptance has had a negative effect on some of the relationships between the older Korean-speaking generation and the younger English-speaking generation who gather for worship in the same space. Although they have separate services, the English-speaking congregation made up of SGKAs is often smaller in size and is expected to fall under the leadership and guidance of the first-generation. First-generation leaders desire to pass down a legacy of worship and theological traditions to the SGKAs, just as they hope to pass down Korean culture and traditions at home. The SGKAs long to find ways of worship and ministry that are meaningful to them in their unique circumstances. With different worldviews and language, misunderstandings and conflict between the two are unavoidable.

One SGKA pastor shared his perspective on the generational conflict in this way:

85. Chung, "Growing up Korean American," 81–82.
86. Jason, interview by author, July 15, 2017.

> They (First-generation Korean church leaders) don't treat us like children, but they see the group as immature, not knowing things as they do, dismissing us by saying, "they just don't know." Our differences are not just seen as differences but as a . . . lack . . . even the term "first generation" and "second generation." It places the first generation first.[87]

Instead of an openness to understand and value the differences, some first-generation leaders see the distinctive SGKAs' worldview as deficient compared to their own. A generational hierarchy is formed because first-generation Korean Americans run the church, fund the building, and hire staff members, excluding SGKAs from any real power within the church. Following Confucian traditions of submission to elders and putting the group before the individual, many first-generation leaders often expect SGKAs to submit to their vision rather than to allow SGKAs and their leaders to voice their own ideas.

With Confucian ideology functioning as a strong foundation within the Korean American church, it is not surprising to see other problematic cultural issues commonly found in the church. One of the biggest issues is the patriarchal repression of women being masked as examples of feminine piety.

Restrictive Gender Roles

Sadly, the Korean American Church is a place of restrictive gender roles that prevent Korean American women of both generations from becoming respected leaders. Mark Hearn writes,

> Both generations largely leave women out of influential leadership and adult teaching roles while relegating them to administrative roles, behind-the-scenes work, or teaching children in Sunday school. Women do not serve in traditional and authoritatively religious roles such as pastor, worship leader, and theological educator whose leadership is often public and in the pulpit.[88]

Women are expected to shoulder much of the sacrifice and hard work of the church, while also displaying obedient submission seen in their quiet dedication. Female pastors, if hired, are seldom given opportunities to

---

87. Interview with a SGKA pastor, November 15, 2017.
88. Hearn, *Religious Experience*, 70.

preach as they are moved to ministries that do the groundwork to support the more visible male leadership.

As a female pastor, I spent over seven years as a children's pastor in one church while other male pastors with less experience have been promoted into higher positions of visible leadership. Some church members and leaders have told me bluntly that if I were not a single woman, I would have been placed in a higher leadership position at the church. It grieves me to see such obvious sexism within this institution. Unfortunately, the Korean American church is slow, if not blind, in seeing and accepting female leaders with qualifications and unique personalities. The silencing of capable women leaders is a critical loss as the church miss out on the unique perspectives and gifts God has given them.

Rose describes her own wounds as a female SGKA in the Korean American church.

> There was a part of me that was like extremely passionate . . . I wanted to be a leader. I had a lot of zeal in me. And, growing up in the Korean church, I always felt that no one offered me the voice to do the things I wanted to do. I felt like, I had so much to offer but I was always stopped or umm, put aside because it wasn't in my place to do those things. I always felt that like my talents and who I was, were being diminished by the leadership or the people above me.[89]

Her desire to serve in the church was quickly silenced and shut down because she did not fit the mold of what serving looks like at a Korean American church. The leadership of her church rejected her suggestions of different ways of doing outreach, and her requests to be a small group leader because of their patriarchal tradition. Feeling misunderstood and rejected, Rose now attends and serves as a leader at a mainline, predominantly white church.

SGKAs grow up seeing women in Korean American churches fill second-tier roles and functions,[90] which is compounded by the teachings of the church in which "women's self-sacrifice and self-denial are reinforced as admirable and considered rewarding."[91] The impact on SGKA women has been an added layer of marginality. They are diminished and rejected by those in authority at the church not only because they are SGKA and younger, but

---

89. Rose, interview by author, July 6, 2017.
90. Son, *Motives of Self-Sacrifice*, 76 and Hong, *Identity, Youth, and Gender*, 27–28.
91. Son, *Motives of Self-Sacrifice*, 77.

also because they are women. It could even be argued that SGKA women live lives of triple marginalization, first from American society for being Korean American, second, from the first- generation for being too Americanized, and finally from Korean American men for being women.

Homecoming: Red Door Ministry as a Place for Wholeness

> He (*sic*) began to have a dim feeling that, to attain his place
> in the world, he must be himself, and not another.[92]
>
> —W. E. B. DU BOIS

Given these experiences of duality, marginality, and homelessness, RDM seeks to provide a place of wholeness where SGKAs can find a place that nurtures the voices that have been suppressed. In *A Hidden Wholeness*, Parker Palmer argues the necessity of creating a space where the voice of the inner teacher, that resides in us all, can guide us from a divided life to a life of wholeness. To be whole and fully engage with themselves and the world around them, SGKAs need to as Du Bois concluded, "be [themselves], and not another." They need a space "where the soul feels safe, [which] will help [them] deal with [their] most divisive issues."[93]

Away from the dual rejection of not being fully Korean or fully American, and far from the pressures to meet the Korean American dream and model minority image of success, RDM is a space that aims to welcome, accept, and understand SGKAs for who they are. This space is designed for SKGAs to "[be] freed to hear [their] own truth, touch what brings [them] joy, become self-critical about [their] faults, and take risky steps toward change—knowing that [they] will be accepted no matter what the outcome."[94] In a space like RDM, SGKAs can create a new sense of self that attests to their resiliency and their creativity.

This chapter has mainly focused on the pains, sufferings, and fragmentations of living a double life. The pulls and tugs of various voices and demands from different cultures have painted a picture in which many in the SGKA population suffer from low self-esteem and self-worth and live a marginal life. Despite the clear negative symptoms of such a divided life,

92. Du Bois, *The Souls of Black Folk*, 11.
93. Palmer, *A Hidden Wholeness*, 65.
94. Palmer, *A Hidden Wholeness*, 60.

psychiatrist Robert J. Lifton describes the possibility of a positive sense of self that could emerge in the description of a protean self:

> We are becoming fluid and many-sided... the protean self emerges from confusion... We feel ourselves buffeted about by unmanageable historical forces and social uncertainties... but rather than collapse under these threats and pulls, the self turns out to be surprisingly resilient. It makes use of bits and pieces here and there and somehow keeps going... We find ourselves evolving a self of many possibilities, one that has risks and pitfalls but at the same time holds out considerable promise for the human future.[95]

The protean self[96] explores the power of human resiliency. This description can be helpful in imagining what an integrated whole SGKA identity can look like as SGKAs bring together "disparate and seemingly incompatible elements of identity,"[97] such as their Korean, American, and religious identities. SGKAs can embark on a life-long "quest for authenticity and meaning, a form-seeking assertion of self"[98] by remaining open and flexible to their various influences while also remaining grounded to themselves.

Palmer also addresses the importance of this combination of remaining connected to others (which he calls *community*) while being fully ourselves (which he calls *solitude*) in the quest for wholeness:

> We have much to learn from within, but it is easy to get lost in the labyrinth of the inner life. We have much to learn from others, but it is easy to get lost in the confusion of the crowd. So we need solitude and community simultaneously: what we learn in one mode can check and balance what we learn in the other. Together, they make us whole, like breathing in and breathing out[99]

RDM is a space where SGKAs can freely breathe! RDM is designed to help SGKAs move toward this wholeness where both solitude and community inform one another in the creation of a new self and a new center. In terms of the themes of homelessness, RDM is one answer in helping SGKAs come home to themselves and create a home in the reality of their double lives. This coming home to themselves and creating a home in their reality of

---

95. Lifton, *The Protean Self*, 1–2.

96. A term that stems from the myth of the wise and prophetic shape shifter, Proteus. Lifton, *The Protean Self*, 5.

97. Lifton, *The Protean Self*, 5.

98. Lifton, *The Protean Self*, 9.

99. Palmer, *A Hidden Wholeness*, 55.

living double lives is done first through exploring and accepting the multiple threads that form the SGKAs' inner self. In a place of acceptance and safety, they can allow their creativity to reframe the way they live in the world around them.

Chapters 3 and 4 are dedicated to the details of how some clients of RDM engage in this journey of self-exploration, self-acceptance, and integration. Chapters 4 and 5 explore how these four clients form new centers from which they reach out to the community. Before hearing the voices of how these four clients experience their continuing homecoming, the space of RDM must be further explained. What makes up a space like RDM? What contexts, theories, and metaphors guide the formation of this space? These are the questions that are answered in chapter 2.

2

The Space of Red Door Ministry

RED DOOR MINISTRY (RDM) is made up of the clients, the counselor, and the space in which they meet. What do the clients and counselor bring to the space? How is the space designed to encourage transformative work? What frameworks and viewpoints help clients to reclaim their voices? As chapter 1 contextualized the background of RDM clients, chapter 2 will examine alternative definitions of space to analyze the theoretical, physical, and internal state (emotional and mental) of the counselor that forms the distinctive space of RDM. First, I turn to postcolonial studies and Homi Bhabha's concept of *third space* to ground the theoretical sphere from which RDM emerged. Next, I trace how the physical space of RDM was imagined, supported, and created. The room is described as a physical reification of D.W. Winnicott's concepts of potential space, transitional object, and holding environment. Finally, in dialogue with various postcolonial and feminist theologians such as Emmanuel Lartey and Grace Ji-Sun Kim, I examine my personal narrative of becoming a whole, empowered woman who can open space within myself to hold the clients' stories and to walk with them in their journeys.

Defining Space

As I consider the various layers that come together to form a unique, culturally sensitive space like RDM, it is imperative that I reflect deeply on how spaces

The Space of Red Door Ministry

are created and experienced. How are spaces conceived? What are the various elements we must consider in creating a space? Once the space is formed, how is it experienced by others? What contributes to their experience?

> The French philosopher Gaston Bachelard once wrote an analysis of what he called the poetics of space. The inside of a house, he said, acquires a sense of intimacy, secrecy, security, real or imagined, because of the experiences that come to seem appropriate for it. The objective space of a house—its corners, corridors, cellar, rooms—is far less important than what poetically it is endowed with, which is usually a quality with an imaginative or figurative value we can name and feel: thus a house may be haunted, or homelike, or prisonlike, or magical. So space acquires emotional and even rational sense by a kind of poetic process, whereby the vacant or anonymous reaches of distance are converted into meaning.[1]

Bachelard's analysis on the poetics of space invites us to see beyond objective space to the poetic, imaginative, emotional, and meaningful. Going beyond architectural trends and function, he emphasizes *experience of space* where we see and feel the space in figurative ways.

Experience of space, therefore, is multilayered. It follows that the creation of space must also be mindful of how we want the space to be experienced. Thoughtful reflection of different layers making up the space of RDM is crucial in understanding how this space functions. To create a space that allows SGKAs to engage in empowering transformations toward wholeness, I must pull from different theories and skillsets and place them together for meaningful experiences to occur. The various definitions of "space" lead us to examine each important layer. The first definition takes us to the theoretical foundations of RDM.

Postcolonial Theory: Creating a Third Space

Space, noun \spās\
the freedom and scope to live, think, and develop in a way that suits one[2]

Referring to the space needed for *all* human beings to grow and flourish on their own terms, this definition shows the basic human necessity of living

---

1. Said. *Orientalism*, 54–55.
2. *Oxford English Dictionary Online*, s.v. "Space, n.1." accessed June 18, 2018.

with freedom and power. In other words, the ability to act, think, and feel freely is essential for human growth. Having that freedom and power taken away stifles our development. The lack of such space in the lives of many SGKAs and other people of color around the world requires a close examination of the origins of such inequality and possible forms of resistance. Postcolonial theory and its influence on pastoral theology provide liberating frameworks that empower the oppressed to identify and overthrow such suffocating forces. Korean North[3] American theologian Grace Ji-Sun Kim explains the space postcolonial theory creates:

> It opens up a place for [the once colonized] to communicate, to develop, and to nurture their own thoughts and ideas. As they experience and embellish this space, it gives them hope as well as opportunity to reevaluate their particular context, situation and life. It is an interpretive act of the descendants of those once subjugated . . . People are in search of full humanity and within these [activities] hope they will be able to find liberation and justice.[4]

The reevaluation of colonial thought and the neocolonial tendencies that continue to exist today, as well as the resurrection of colonized voices, recover the freedom and power that was once taken away by dominant forces. We now turn to examine the source of colonialism and the notion of Western superiority.

Starting from Orientalism: Labeling the "Other"

Edward Said

Palestinian American scholar Edward Said traces the prejudiced attitudes which served as the underlying belief that led to global colonization of the "Orient"[5] by the West.

> The essential relationship, on political, cultural, and even religious grounds, was seen—in the West . . .—to be one between a strong and a weak partner . . . The Oriental is irrational, depraved (fallen),

---

3. Her qualifier.
4. Kim. *Holy Spirit, Chi,* 70.
5. Said uses this term to describe how Western Europe has historically described the East, mostly to refer to what is currently called the Middle East, and other nations where Islam is the main religion. For our purposes, the term "orient" can be extended to encompass Asian, African, and Latin American countries that the West colonized.

childlike, "different;" thus the European is rational, virtuous, mature, "normal."[6]

By drawing a clear distinction between the West and the non-West, the rationalization of "Western superiority and Oriental inferiority"[7] became more concrete. Historically, the "Orient" had become the "deepest and most recurring images of the Other"[8] for the West. By labeling difference and otherness as inferior, the West has perpetuated "an uneven exchange"[9] with the "Orient." European powers invaded these nations on the basis that they are bringing rationality, virtue, maturity, and "normalcy" to those whom they saw as an "irrational, depraved (fallen), childlike, 'different'" other. The history of colonialism shows that such imperialistic actions led to the rationalization of the exploitation of non-Western countries.

This colonial belief of Western superiority persists in the pernicious injustices of racism, classism, and sexism in our society today. These injustices are justified by depriving the "other" of their full humanity and flattening them with destructive stereotypes. This form of oppression continues to be perpetuated by the media and literature as they make harmful generalizations of the "other." Said uses the depictions of Muslims in American media and literature as an example. These portrayals "in modern American awareness of the Arab or Islamic Orient [are] to keep the region and its people conceptually emasculated, reduced to 'attitudes,' 'trends,' statistics: in short, dehumanized."[10]

Dehumanization often leads to objectification, where we see fellow human beings simplified as fulfillers of roles or objects on which we project our anxieties and fears of difference. People of color around the globe, including SGKAs in the United States, intimately know the pains of being stereotyped and dehumanized by the "dominant gaze." Colonial thought persists in American society when white and non-white groups of people view anyone outside of their own group, such as SGKAs, as perpetual foreigners. This kind of oppression and dehumanization creates a sense of emergency within those who are exempt from full participation in society.

6. Said, *Orientalism*, 40.
7. Said, *Orientalism*, 42.
8. Said, *Orientalism*, 1.
9. Said, *Orientalism*, 12.
10. Said, *Orientalism*, 291.

Opening the Red Door
Postcolonial Critique
Homi Bhabha

"The state of emergency is also always a state of *emergence*."[11]

—HOMI BHABHA

Edward Said's work uncovers the notion of Western superiority by tracing its presence throughout history and literature. He does not, however, suggest how the stereotyped and objectified "other" can reclaim their humanity in such deeply rooted systems of oppression. Said "describe[s] a particular system of ideas not by any means to displace the system with a new one . . . [He] attempted to raise a whole set of questions that are relevant in discussing the problems of human experience."[12] Postcolonial theory seeks to continue the critique and to creatively craft solutions that challenge this system of ideas.

Indian English scholar Homi Bhabha contributes in creating a space of resistance against colonialism in postcolonial theory. The emergency of stifling injustices and the belittling of non-Western cultures and people push postcolonial critique and postcolonial spaces to emerge. Bhabha sees postcolonialism as "bear[ing] witness to the unequal and uneven forces of cultural representation"[13] as well as "elaborating strategies . . . that initiate new signs of identity, and innovative sites of collaboration, and contestation, in the act of defining the idea of society itself."[14] Identifying the inequalities of colonialism is not enough to bring about the breathable space all human beings need for individual and societal growth. Bhabha draws attention to the process and to unique "'in between spaces"[15] that aid in the redefinition of self, community, and culture that reclaims the humanity and authentic cultures of those formerly colonized.

Pastoral theologian Emmanuel Lartey further explains what this postcolonial process and space must do for equal and just interactions: "The task postcolonializing activities seek to accomplish entails critique, validation, recovery, and construction. They aim to facilitate the formerly

---

11. Bhabha, *Location of Culture*, 59.
12. Said, *Orientalism*, 325.
13. Bhabha, *Location of Culture*, 245.
14. Bhabha, *Location of Culture*, 2.
15. Bhabha, *Location of Culture*, 2.

colonized person's authentic participation in intercultural engagement."[16] This multilayered process that postcolonialism necessitates, demands radically new perspectives and transformations on existing oppressive systems, on sense of self, and on views of the future. Engaging in the postcolonial process is a messy ordeal that does not follow a neat step-by-step order. Critique, validation, recovery, and construction occur simultaneously or within one another. For the sake of clarification, these steps will be explored each in turn in the next section.

Postcolonial Process

Critique of Oppressive Systems

The process of decolonizing must be grounded in the critique of oppressive systems and of the damaging identifications of the colonized that are in place. We can return to stereotypes as an example of oppressive practice and identification. To resist the damaging stereotypes and dehumanizing gaze of the colonizer, the inaccuracy of such identification must be unveiled:

> The stereotype is not a simplification because it is a false representation of a given reality. It is a simplification because it is an arrested, fixated form of representation that, in denying the play of difference (which the negation through the Other permits) constitutes problem for the *representation* of the subject in significations of psychic and social relations.[17]

This fixed form of representation does not do justice to the ever-changing, growing selves of full humans. Such harmful stereotypes not only damage the relationship between the colonizer and the colonized but also have injurious effects on the personhood of the one who is stereotyped. Living with the stereotype without resistance can "introduce alienation into our sense of self. We need to break free from this alienation."[18] For authentic connection to self and to others, we must break through the alienating wall of dehumanizing stereotypes. The deeply embedded assumption of Western norms and viewpoints as the main narrative must be broken down by the addition and validation of colonized voices.

---

16. Lartey, "Postcolonializing Pastoral Theology," 80.
17. Bhabha, *Location of Culture*, 107.
18. Huddart, *Homi K Bhabha*, 29–30.

Opening the Red Door

Validation of Full Humanity

Asian Americans are often stereotyped as being silent, nonthreatening, and smart, which stems from the image of the "model minority."[19] This stereotyping must be critiqued, and a validation of their full humanity, including their gifts, contributions, and unique positions, must be made. SGKAs, like other Asian Americans and people of color who have been colonized, must validate who they are by defining and developing themselves "in a way that suits one."[20] They must see themselves as people of value whose experiences and voices are equally important and in need of representation in intercultural discourse. Validation happens when the "agency of the colonized [is recognized as they] . . . articulate and assert their dignity, self-worth, and identity and . . . empower themselves."[21] The colonized can validate their own identities and experiences by narrating their own stories. By refusing to let dominant forces define them, SKGAs and other colonized people can become the authors and translators of their own lives. This type of validation must be protected. "When you fail to protect the right to narrate, you are in danger of filling the silence with . . . hectoring voices carried by loudspeakers from podiums of great height over people who shrink into indistinguishable masses."[22] Each voice must be validated as a valuable truth that adds depth and color to our intercultural understanding of one another.

Recovery through Reclamation

Recovery often starts with reclaiming the past cultures, histories, and traditions of the colonized that the West had deemed inferior, insignificant, or immoral:

> What is required is to demonstrate another territory of translation, another testimony of analytical argument, a different engagement . . . we must rehistoricize . . . This can only happen if we relocate the referential and institutional demands of such theoretical work in the field of cultural difference.[23]

---

19. See chapter 1 for critique of this stereotype.
20. *Oxford English Dictionary Online*, s.v. "Space, n.1." accessed June 18, 2018.
21. Lartey, "Postcolonializing Pastoral Theology," 81–82.
22. Bhabha, "On Writing Rights," 140.
23. Bhabha, *Location of Culture*, 47.

The Space of Red Door Ministry

Rather than using Western ideas as the "normative" ground from which all other cultures are translated, the colonized must reorient themselves within their own history and traditions.

Grace Ji-Sun Kim gives us an example of recovery in the formation of an Asian American theology on the Holy Spirit. She starts with the Eastern concept of *chi* and how Korean and other Asian Christians can enrich their view of the Holy Spirit by recovering the vital role of *chi* in the Eastern understanding of life: "Chi is crucial for our livelihood and to realize that Chi is the Spirit in all things. This Spirit is the same spirit of God."[24] Pulling from the ancient concept of *chi* dating back to the Yin era (1751–1112 BCE)[25] in Chinese history, Kim reclaims the value and meaning of *chi* before the arrival of Western influence. Her exploration and utilization of *chi* to form a new, richer understanding of the spirit of God for Asian Americans, Korean Americans included, depict the importance of recovering and reclaiming the traditions of the colonized. Kim's intercultural pneumatology, described in more detail in chapter 4, also exhibits construction, the final stage in the postcolonial process.

Construction of New Realities

Lartey explains how a postcolonial reality, and for our purposes space, is constructed:

> Subjugated knowledge needs to be re-appropriated, validated, and put to work in the construction of new realities, theories, and practices able to forge a new consciousness and new orientation to life for all in the future. Postcolonial thought thus requires both courage and creativity.[26]

Postcolonial construction does not only challenge Western thought by drawing from the indigenous cultures that were colonized, but it also takes heed of the postcolonial process itself in the creation of the new. Courage allows for confrontations of the oppressive systems in place and creativity brings about new "realities, theories, and practices." Grace Ji-sun Kim courageously and creatively analyzes the Eastern concept of *chi* and the Western Christian beliefs of the Holy Spirit. She critiques the rigid pneumatology of

---

24. Kim. *Holy Spirit, Chi*, 30.
25. Kim. *Holy Spirit, Chi*, 10.
26. Lartey, "Postcolonializing Pastoral Theology," 81.

Western Christianity that left no room for Eastern spiritual understandings of life and its source. Kim, a Christian herself, does not simply dismiss Western influences for the sake of affirming Eastern ones but, through critique, validation, and recovery, constructs a new understanding of God's spirit that holds deeper meaning and relevance for Asian Christians. She uses her own hybridity to form a new theology. Where can this kind of liberating and empowering postcolonial process take place? The critique, validation, and recovery of various cultures are constructed in what Bhabha calls *third space*.

Postcolonial Space

Third Space and Hybridity

Kim explains third space:

> Bhabha's third space emerges from an analytical scrutiny of diverse cultures rather than from integrating them. This is an invaluable space where one creates and reimagines. It will be in this space that positive discourse can occur and where people can dialogue with one another and recognize the gift of the Other.[27]

Engaging in postcolonial thought brings us to a place of tension. Although we critique colonial narratives and Western normativity, we cannot deny its history and influence, embedded in our formation and in our society. At the same time, we cannot go back to a precolonial mindset as if colonialism and imperialism did not occur. The reality of many people of color, SGKAs included, is one of tension and double living (discussed in chapter 1). To participate in the process of postcolonialism, we must carve out and claim a space that affirms our experiences as complex and full human beings who are formed by a variety of cultures. This space, being "neither the One nor the Other but something else besides, which contests the terms and territories of both,"[28] describes the creative, messiness of third space.

Bhabha recognizes that there are "more complex cultural . . . boundaries that exist on the cusp of these often opposed [first and third world] . . . spheres."[29] The lines separating the colonizer and the colonized may not be

---

27. Kim, *Holy Spirit, Chi*, 100.
28. Bhabha, *Location of Culture*, 41.
29. Bhabha, *Location of Culture*, 248.

The Space of Red Door Ministry

as clearly drawn. In the same way, SGKAs' identities and social locations are muddled and complex. For SGKAs, a *hybridity* of various cultural spheres are mingled. "Hybridity is not about the dissolution of differences but about renegotiating the structure of power built on differences. The differences should not be viewed negatively, but welcomed as places of potential imagination and rebirth."[30] This hybridity births a creative space, a third space out of which emerges a sense of agency, imagination, and uniqueness. By living on the edge of different cultures, "we are in a position to translate the differences between them into a kind of solidarity."[31] Bhabha invites the colonized to use their hybridity as a foundation to raise their voices.

Bhabha's often esoteric writing style, as well as the refusal to reach a clear and definitive description that is easy to grasp, gives voice to the messy, multilayered, and nuanced thoughts and feelings some SGKAs and other colonized people may hold within them. Feeling stuck between cultures and generations and not fitting the traditional, expected roles of gender and race, SGKAs need to create a literal and figurative third space that draws from their hybridity.

Red Door Ministry as Third Space

RDM is the external third space resulting from the figurative and internal third space SGKAs need for reclaiming their full humanity. Nothing within the space is set in meaning or in process. Each person, each item within the space, and each time the client and I come together, new translations and new perspectives take place:

> It is that Third Space, though unrepresentable in itself, which constitutes the discursive conditions of enunciation that ensure that the meaning and symbols of culture have no primordial unity or fixity; that even the same signs can be appropriated, translated, rehistoricized and read anew.[32]

This constant flux and reimagining of meaning and symbols helps RDM to be the open and flexible space SGKA clients need. They bring their own set of various cultural meanings and symbols. It is "the in-between space, which questions established categorizations of culture and identity and

---

30. Kim, *Holy Spirit, Chi*, 96.
31. Bhabha, *Location of Culture*, 244.
32. Bhabha, *Location of Culture*, 55.

opens up the possibilities of renegotiating power and creating new cultural means."[33] With a foundation of compassion, love, and acceptance, this space acknowledges the hybridity stemming from the interactions of the client and the counselor, the hybridity of multiple cultural formations, and the hybrid roles as both oppressed and oppressor/colonized and colonizer found within us.[34]

RDM is a space for confrontation and self-critique where amid tensions, individuals find transformation in reclaiming their voices. RDM as third space gives SGKA clients the room to courageously and creatively claim their "freedom and scope to live, think, and develop in a way that suits"[35] them. This space allows for "liberating human activity, in line with divine activity,"[36] which can have communal and societal ramifications. To add to our understanding of RDM as liberating third space, the physical space of the room must also be considered.

Imagined Space to Physical Space

Space, noun \spās\
physical extent or area; extent in two or three dimensions[37]

A second definition of space takes us to the physical room of RDM. Starting from its conception as an imagined space, we move to the process of creating this room within a Korean American church. The physical details of the room's layout and objects are explained through the lens of Winnicott's theories of potential space, transitional object, and holding environment.

Envisioning Red Door Ministry

In my first semester as a Th.D. student, I entered my advisor's office expecting a standard conversation on course selection and strategies to excel in the program. To my surprise, he led me through an imaginative exercise that thrust me years into the future. I envisioned a counseling space set apart by

33. Kim, *Embracing the Other,* 57.
34. The dual roles of colonizer and colonized is further analyzed within my personal narrative in the last section of this chapter.
35. *Oxford English Dictionary Online,* s.v. "Space, n.1." accessed June 18, 2018.
36. Lartey, "Postcolonializing Pastoral Theology," 94.
37. *Oxford English Dictionary Online,* s.v. "Space, n.1." accessed June 18, 2018.

a bold red door. With my eyes closed, I allowed my voice, guided by the Holy Spirit, to articulate a vision of a culturally sensitive counseling space.

Behind the red door with a golden handle was a sacred space where people in pain would be embraced by love, compassion, and forgiveness. In this dream state, a child asked, "Why is the door red?" Having worked as a children's pastor, I bent over to look the child in the eyes and explained, "The red symbolizes the blood of the lamb. People are safe from judgment and punishment." With holy imagination, I continued to describe the room's layout. There was a large plush couch under a print of Georges Seurat, a French Impressionist known for painting outdoor social scenes of various people and places. The walls were a calm gray blue that created a feeling of peace. In my mind's eye, I saw myself sitting with different people, young and old, rich and poor, individuals and groups, similar to the array of people found in Seurat's paintings. When my eyelids opened, forty-five minutes after I had first closed my eyes, my advisor invited me to "Go! Write this down, see where God takes you with this."

Creating Red Door Ministry: Under Construction

Two years after the initial waking dream, the church I served as children's pastor gave me the space and resources to make this vision a reality. As one of the largest Korean American church in the southeastern part of the United States, this church had the resources and the openness to support this new venture. In the beginning, the head pastor strongly supported the vision behind the proposed counseling space, bringing the church session on board. Many church members, including the elders and staff members, showed excitement about the prospect of pastoral care and counseling within the church. Because the Korean American church serves as the location for meeting most of the social, cultural, and emotional needs of the Korean American community, having a counseling space within church walls seemed logical.

The sudden death of the head pastor only four months after RDM had opened sent waves of uncertainty, shock, and insecurity throughout the entire church, and RDM was not immune. Without the powerful support this space once enjoyed from the charismatic leader of the church, pressures to prove the need for this space emerged. Not fully understanding the concept of confidentiality, the church session and other leaders asked for information about clients as a way to justify the effectiveness and need for the ministry. I felt the need to defend the importance of RDM as I walked the thin line of educating the church leaders on the nature of counseling and confidentiality as well as sharing information, in general terms, about the experiences of transformation that I witnessed in the lives of clients. The support from staff remained, but given RDM's unique identity, many church leaders and congregation members struggled to understand how RDM fell in line with the overall mission and vision of the church. The room itself is located on the margins of the church campus. Tucked away at the end of the hall in one of the five buildings on campus, its location on the edge of the church seems to mimic the marginal existence of the clients and the counselor.

Inside the Room

Creating Potential Space

The physical space of RDM is designed to encourage the creation of a safe, trusting *potential space* that object relations theorist D.W. Winnicott felt necessary "for creative playing and for cultural experience."[38] A person's ability to creatively and spontaneously respond to a given situation or relationship signifies a healthy development of the self that stems from a trusting space:

> This potential space between baby and mother, between child and family, between individual and society or the world, depends on experience which leads to trust. It can be looked upon as sacred to the individual in that it is here that the individual experiences creative living. By contrast, exploitation of this area leads to a pathological condition in which the individual is cluttered up with persecutory elements of which he (sic) has no means to ridding himself.[39]

To usher in freedom, agency, and creativity in the lives of the clients, the physical space itself had to embody such values through its aesthetics. I painted the walls and chose the furniture to align with the vivid vision I had in my advisor's office two years earlier. The desks, bookcases, lamps, artwork, and the finishing touches were all intentionally chosen to create a place of welcome, peace, and freedom. Each object was to contribute to

---

38. Winnicott, *Playing and Reality*, 144.
39. Winnicott, *Playing and Reality*, 139.

The Space of Red Door Ministry

the aesthetics of the space that would be conducive to the formation of a trusting, holding environment.

For example, one will notice that many of the artworks or objects in the room are images of birds. Birds can symbolize freedom and beauty. It is my desire to see each client spread their wings and soar majestically and triumphantly through their lives. I also light a candle at the beginning of my day in RDM to represent the presence of the Holy Spirit in the room. The warm glow of the candle may not light the entire room, but its flickering flame adds to the ambiance by welcoming in new sources of life.

A large whiteboard hangs on the wall next to the couch. Surprisingly, three of the clients mentioned that this whiteboard was a helpful tool for them. As a visually oriented teacher and learner, I use the whiteboard to draw out what the clients say with words and images. Clients have stated the external visualizing of their internal thoughts and feelings helps them to better understand and grasp what they are confronting. Rose explained,

> What I appreciate is this whiteboard. It's very easy for me to understand how my heart works and [I] become more self-aware when you use the whiteboard . . . I'm very much of an organizational type, so really when you use the white board, like it just feeds my soul. I'm like, "Wow! This is exactly [it]," sometimes I just go straight home and just write down everything . . . the same way that you just did.[40]

When asked her opinion about the negatives of the space, Rose joked, "The whiteboard could be longer."[41]

Jason also offered his opinion about the whiteboard and its centrality to the space. He shared, "I think a lot of the board work was important, like visualizing things. I think it was super important to me because it took things out of my mind and kind of put it on a piece of paper."[42] Charting their concerns on the whiteboard, not only helps clients to see their complaints more clearly, but it also serves as a visual aid for them to challenge old notions and break down oppressive ideas.

Ava provided a thoughtful metaphor about the whiteboard's usage, "it's kind of like opening [the] door. Um, I had a lot of . . . boundaries, I didn't know they were walls. I just had a set mind of thinking. [When using the board,] everything makes sense or just clicks, I just feel like . . . we

---

40. Rose, interview by author, July 6, 2017.
41. Rose, interview by author, July 6, 2017.
42. Jason, interview by author, July 15, 2017.

dissect everything."[43] The whiteboard functions as a liberating object that aids clients in processing information. It also serves as a creative plaything that allows clients to courageously confront fears and oppressive notions that previously seemed to be overwhelming in their abstractions. The whiteboard has become an object through which clients find their agency and power as constricting boundaries and walls open to a new understanding of themselves.

Transitional Object

The whiteboard, and by extension the entire room of RDM, can function as a transitional object for the clients as they move toward forming their own voice and strengthening their sense of self. Winnicott describes the function of a transitional object:

> It is not the object, of course, that is transitional. The object represents the infant's transition from a state of being merged with the mother to a state of being in relation to the mother as something outside and separate.[44]

The "mother" for many of the clients is the embedded oppressive notions of self and the pressures placed by their parents and society that make many of them feel they are not acceptable as who they are. Using the whiteboard and other interactions within the walls of RDM represent the transition the clients are making from trying to become the ideal their parents and society have set for them to placing themselves "outside and separate" from this prewritten narrative to be the author of their own stories. This transition does not cut the "mother" from the client's lives. Instead, it seeks newer, healthier ways for them to relate to their parents and communities, while validating their own selves.

Many RDM clients enter with a fragmented sense of self that stems from their double lives as people living between different cultures. The whiteboard and the space "promise to the [client] an experience where the unintegrations of self find integrations through the form provided by the transformational object."[45] Clients make their way toward wholeness

---

43. Ava, interview by author, July 5, 2017.
44. Winnicott, *Playing and Reality*, 19–20.
45. Bollas, "Aesthetic Moment," 41.

The Space of Red Door Ministry

through the frame provided by RDM, a transitional object that allows them to reclaim who they are through key experiences with and within the space.

Experiencing a Holding Environment

Two clients reflected on other objects in the physical space that are important elements for personal change. Ava explains: "I just feel so relaxed here and I feel like [that relaxation is] immediately broken once I walk out that door . . . maybe it's the colors. It's very soothing and, yeah, you just feel like a person."[46] RDM as a transitional object and potential space provides relaxation and comfort to Ava who finds safety and trust in the space and with the counselor. She feels that the space and the counselor embrace her with acceptance and freedom. In Winnicott's words, Ava's experience of RDM is "an area not challenged, because no claim is made on its behalf except that it shall exist as a resting place for the individual."[47] The general sense of welcome and safety experienced by all those who enter RDM become personalized as clients like Ava start to identify the space as a holding environment where they feel safe and free to develop their unique voices.

Sam shares similar sentiments when he states, "it's just like a very cozy, safe environment . . . it's like cottage-y . . . the furniture, the flowers, the not-so-overpowering lights and even just like sitting here talking to you, you have a very soft voice . . . there's no judgment here."[48] I was intrigued that what started out as a description of the space for both eventually turned into a description of their experience of me, their counselor. I had become an extension of the space. It seemed the clients did not separate the physical space from the physical person who created the space. Another way to look at it is that I, the counselor, worked in tandem with the other objects in the room to make up their overall experience of the physical environment.

The clients can experience me as a real, safe person without judgment because I am able to open up space within my internal self to hold them in their progress. Their transformations are possible because of "the sensation–based emotional state of being gently, sturdily wrapped in the arms of the mother"[49] that I demonstrate. This act and environment of holding

---

46. Ava, interview by author, July 5, 2017.
47. Winnicott, *Playing and Reality*, 3.
48. Sam, interview by author, June 29, 2017.
49. Ogden, "On Holding and Containing," 143.

must have "the sense of continuity of being sustained over time"[50] because clients are in different developmental stages in their lives. Winnicott reveals the goal of creating this holding environment:

> If I do this well enough the patient will find his or her own self and will be able to exist and to feel real. Feeling real is more than existing; it is finding a way to exist as oneself, and to relate to objects as oneself, and to have a self into which to retreat for relaxation . . . it is not easy, and it is emotionally exhausting. But we get our rewards. Even when our patients do not get cured they are grateful to us for seeing them as they are, and this gives us a satisfaction of a deep kind.[51]

We will unpack the clients' experiences of finding themselves in their own voice in chapter 3. For the remainder of this chapter, however, I will examine what kind of inner work I must do to hold my clients "well enough." As a pastoral counselor, I can sustain this kind of environment only by constantly reexamining myself and working on my own self-acceptance to authentically join the clients in their journeys. It is at this crossroads of our two paths toward health and discovery where honest work between two real people can lead to sacred changes.

Counselor's Inner Space

> *Space,* noun \spās\
> mental sphere within which a person lives or operates; a notional region private to an individual within which he or she feels comfortable or unrestricted[52]

> *Space,* noun \spās\
> a continuous area or expanse which is free, available and unoccupied[53]

These last two definitions of space guide us through my own mental space as the counselor and the work I had to do to claim my own voice. It also points to what I must continuously do to be free and available for my clients. I cannot separate who I am from my role as pastoral counselor. As such, an

---

50. Ogden, "On Holding and Containing," 118.
51. Winnicott, *Playing and Reality*, 158.
52. *Oxford English Dictionary Online*, s.v. "Space, n.1." accessed June 18, 2018.
53. *Oxford English Dictionary Online*, s.v. "Space, n.1." accessed June 18, 2018.

exploration of my identity, as well as the various cultural and contextual influences on my formation, will shed light on the valuable tools I bring into my counseling work at RDM. The first step is to identify the shared experiences that I have with clients and the distinctions that differentiate us.

The Counselor as Like All Others, Like Some Others, Like No Other

In his book, *In Living Color: An Intercultural Approach to Pastoral Care and Counseling,* Lartey draws from Kluckholn and Murray's "formulation of human personhood"[54] from 1948 that we are "like all others, like some others, like no other." [55] This simple phrase captures the complexities of relating to other human beings and serves as the foundation for my approach to pastoral care and counseling. On a base level, I experience and hold certain values that are shared by all others. Values such as love, freedom, safety, and power are universal. In the vastness of *humanity*, I am one of *all*, [one] who "feel[s], experience[s], and know[s] ... [and shares the] basic human characteristics, needs, and emotions that form a bond of common human experience."[56] As I understand myself better, I can appreciate and respect the personal journey each human being takes in her/his life.

As a person of color, I am part of a group whose race has elicited unfair, discriminatory treatment from oppressive systems that prize white Americans. Easily stereotyped because of my "otherness," I know what it feels like to be stripped of my multi-dimensionality and seen as a flat stereotype. Like *some* other Korean Americans, I am in a constant state of negotiating between the Western values of the United States, the country of my citizenship, and the Eastern values of Korea, the country of my heritage. As a Korean American, I am like *some* others who have the same cultural background, including the shared traumas, celebrations, and history of a people who have been oppressed and liberated and torn apart by colonialization and war, the impact of which remains to this day. I draw strength from the similarities I share with other Korean Americans who have immigrated to a foreign, often unwelcoming, land to not just survive but to flourish. As a Korean American woman, I also share in the experience of patriarchy with other Korean American women who were raised in patriarchal Confucian

---

54. Lartey, *In Living Color*, 34.
55. Lartey, *In Living Color*, 34.
56. Cooper-White, *Many Voices*, 49.

homes. Lastly, as a Korean American Christian woman, I share in the faith and hope of *some* other women who turn to God as the source of our inspiration for redemption and liberation from such hardships and oppression.

I am unique, however, in my formation. Unlike the SGKAs in this study, I was born in South Korea. My family left South Korea when I was four years old so my father could be a missionary. My father's work took my family to live in several Southeast Asian countries. I had a distinctive education that spanned both public and private schools in Singapore, Malaysia, the Philippines, and the United States. Some of these schools offered lessons in several different languages. Exposure to these various cultures and languages helped me understand from a young age that cultural and linguistic differences are not to be feared or diminished but rather valued. These differences can, in fact, add a richness to viewpoints, meanings, and understandings of the world.

By holding onto the truth that I am like all others, some others, and no other, I can uphold the human dignity of each of my clients and meet them with respect and empathy. This framework helps me carve out a "mental sphere within which [I] operate,"[57] where I feel comfortable and unrestricted in the similarities and differences I have with my clients. A further exploration of my unique formation and journey toward wholeness sheds light to the space created within me as I counsel SGKA clients.

Pushing Past Labels

Reframing the "Rebellious Child"

From early childhood, a curiosity and creativity emerged within me that clashed with cultural norms and Confucian standards that socialized me. My father did not know how to name this uniqueness within me, and he therefore labeled me "the rebellious child." Constantly silenced for speaking out and asking questions, my father saw and treated me as a disrespectful and difficult daughter. I felt unwanted and unwelcomed. I was a bad daughter.

I realize now that despite the pain it caused me to have such a curious mind, I am like no other, a fact to be celebrated and not suppressed. Rather than hide my unique formation and remain deferential to fit the cultural expectation of Korean American women, I

---

57. *Oxford English Dictionary Online*, s.v. "Space, n.1." accessed June 18, 2018.

The Space of Red Door Ministry

> ... truly need to articulate [my] experience and claim [my] space as participant in the act of liberation. [I] need to act as [an] agent of change and work towards a new future where women can claim their true humanity and be liberated from the numerous bonds of oppression.[58]

To help others claim their own voices and freedom from oppressive forces, I must first assert my own "space as [a] participant in the act of liberation" within my life. My curiosities and creativity must be seen as gifts and my experiences seen as fuel that fires them into action.

I have reframed my father's label of "rebellious" with other words such as "reforming," "resourceful," and "re-imagining" that accurately affirm these qualities. My father was not the only one to label me. The Korean American community was and continues to be quick in labeling and categorizing me.

1.5 Generation: A Fluid Identity

Many people in my Korean American community place me in the middle of the first and second generation and categorize me as part of the 1.5 generation.[59] In many ways, they are accurate in doing so. Sophia Park defines the 1.5 generation as those who are "bilingual and bicultural. Being in-between and in both the Korean and Western culture ... function[ing] as a bridge, becoming a connecting point in the multicultural context of America."[60] Park claims that the 1.5 generation is in a unique position to contribute to both cultures by forming a new space. They are "seen as both an outsider and an insider who can connect others, creating together a new dynamic space where there is no inside or outside."[61] RDM is one such dynamic space that results from my existence as both outsider and insider.

My own experience with 1.5 generation Korean Americans, however, has led me to think that this label does not fully capture the essence of who I am. When I first arrived in the United States at the age of eleven, I realized that I belonged neither to the SGKAs who were born here or to the 1.5 generation Korean Americans who emigrated directly from South Korea. Having left Korea before entering preschool, I could not relate to the culture

58. Kim, *Grace of Sophia*, 19.
59. Park, "1.5 Generation," 230–42.
60. Park, "1.5 Generation," 232.
61. Park, "1.5 Generation," 240–41.

and norms of other Korean immigrants. In the past, I have often joked by saying I am a 1.7 or 1.8 generation rather than being part of the 1.5 generation. This designation is due to my lack of immersion in and understanding of Korean culture. I assumed that I must be more Americanized than the other 1.5 Korean Americans because my command of Korean culture was not as strong or as fluent as theirs. Neither fitting the mold of a SGKA nor a 1.5 generation, I felt like an anomaly who did not belong to any subgroup within the Korean American community. Rather than stay in this space of confusion and loneliness, I came to embrace the fact that I

> ... have a unique but fluid identity. And, as [I] live in this special in-between space, which is a liberating space where creativity and empowerment can be found ... [I] can be an immensely creative and healing force in a cultural milieu that seems to be entering into a state of "permanent liminality" characterized by constant and accelerating change.[62]

Kim's description of people living in in-between spaces challenges me to draw from all the borders that press against me. Using my curiosity and creativity, I can use my complex identity as a tool to help others navigate their own complexities and transformations.

Claiming My Voice

A New Definition of Culture

As I have clarified my identity and heightened my awareness of my cultural and social location over the last few years, I have realized that no number can fully capture who I am as a Korean American. In defining my own identity, I have found affirmation in anthropologist and psychotherapist Karen Seeley's redefinition of culture:

> Many psychotherapists continue to conceive of culture as a unitary entity that belongs to the social group, rather than to the individual, that is located in the external world of materials and products rather than within the internal word of thoughts, emotions, and ideas, and that is embodied in group ritual and custom rather than in individual action.[63]

---

62. Kim, *Holy Spirit, Chi*, 87.
63. Seeley, *Cultural Psychotherapy*, 71.

This alternate view of culture as residing in the individual freed me from trying to fit into a cultural mold of one group or another. The culture I belong to resides in my own internal world of thoughts, emotions, and ideas. This new definition coupled with encouragement from my professors, therapists, and mentors led me to accept more of myself and to see value in my unique formation. I now feel freer to hear and speak my own voice. This was not always the case. Most of my life I found myself being silenced: unseen and unheard. The process of climbing out of silence took place in multiple areas of my life.

Climbing Out of Silence

Upon my arrival to the United States, my voice had been silenced countless times because I was a young Korean American woman. Those doing the silencing had mostly been white Westerners or Korean men. For the sake of feeling accepted and belonging in various social locations, I presented myself as a high-performing, socially likeable person who could adapt to the many roles and stereotypes that were placed upon me.

In school, I received good grades because I excelled at digesting information and applying it as truth without much question. I automatically assumed that the work of Western philosophers, theorists, and theologians being taught were superior in their knowledge and possessed more valuable and truthful ideas than the philosophers, theorists, and theologians who shared similar experiences or backgrounds with me. Whenever I was asked to critique a theory or concept, I made sure my critique aligned with those I heard from the professor or other well-established theorists. It was not until my first Th.D. course when a professor helped me realize that my voice was missing in my papers. His comment still rings clearly in my mind: "This is well written, but where is *your* voice? I know what these people are saying; I want to know what *you* think." He empowered me to speak and write my own thoughts, and he gave me the confidence to imbue my words with the same value and consideration that I gave to other scholars. For the first time, I felt permitted to create and view the world from my own perspective and experiences.

When I left school and went to church, I served silently in the background as the obedient, hardworking Sunday school teacher and children's pastor. I lived into the expectations and one-dimensional view of piety and holiness that young Korean American women must embody within the set culture of our church community. In time, I found the freedom and power to try out new ideas and to speak my voice out loud. This was only possible because the church I served was one of the largest Korean American churches in the area, leaving the male church leaders preoccupied with other matters. I was left alone to do what I wished within my own department, but I also felt neglected when I needed help. As I stepped into roles of more visible leadership, I struggled with having my voice heard and my ideas executed. Although I had the support of fellow staff members, my ideas were often rejected and required extended explanation by the ones making the final decision. I feel as though I had to fight for every inch of space in RDM.

Beyond the academy and the church, I also had to move beyond silence in romantic relationships. The patriarchal voices of my culture taught me that as long as I served the man and he was happy, I was a good partner. Even when I was abused emotionally, physically, and sexually, my role was to serve. Grace Ji-Sun Kim's account of the Korean North American women rang true:

> Korean North American women feel a great deal of alienation and loneliness. In addition to being members of a marginalized Asian North American subculture . . . women often experience the frustration of not having their experiences recognized, validated, and supported by men within their own ethnic communities. Thus they are doubly alienated.[64]

In multiple points of past relationships, I recall not being able to recognize my own voice. In this sense, I felt alienated threefold. I was alienated from mainstream American culture, from the men I was dating, and from my own voice. I simply did not have thoughts or opinions I could claim or call my own. Even when I spoke, I barely recognized my voice. My fear of not being taken seriously, ridiculed, punished, or completely ignored turned down the volume of my voice until I was muted. I was terribly unhappy and exhausted from trying to be who others wanted me to be. With the help of mentors, therapists, professors, supervisors, and friends who created a nonthreatening, nurturing space, I slowly started to pay attention and listen to my own voice. In their company, I learned to value my voice and to speak out more clearly.

---

64. Kim, *Grace of Sophia*, 75.

The Space of Red Door Ministry

Being True to Self

As I reclaimed my voice, I started to see the importance of authenticity and of revealing my truth, motivating me to do all things more honestly and with purpose. I discovered that living life more authentically adds a unique spin on things. This may mean I do not perfectly meet the unbending expectations that others set as acceptable or good. In reflecting authenticity, I am reminded of my college days when a friend taught me to play a guitar. I had difficulty learning how to strum, even when I had a good grasp of the rhythm of a song. My friend continually told me to find the "Jinny-strum" and to stop trying to imitate or follow other musicians' strumming patterns. Developing my "authentic strum" required some unlearning of set strum patterns and unhearing of the technical aspects of the song. To discover my strum, I focused on the beauty of the song and let the music flow from within. In doing so, I found the "Jinny-strum" that felt and sounded natural. Homi Bhabha describes the authenticity of being true to self in a similar way:

> To be true to a self, one must learn to be a little untrue, out-of-joint with the signification of cultural generalizability . . . sing a little out of tune; just fail to hit the top E in James Boon' *Aida* effect . . . the truth lie[s]—always a little beside the point.[65]

To be an authentic and personable pastoral counselor with integrity, I must continue to self-critically reflect, unhearing and unlearning the set parameters of what I learned to be the acceptable way of doing counseling. This "out-of-joint" authenticity is not lost on the clients. Ava claims:

Ava: You just feel like a person.

Interviewer/author: Your previous therapists didn't feel like a person?

Ava: No.

Interviewer: What did they feel like?

Ava: They just seemed like very, just robotic . . . I just felt like they just went and like did the checklist . . . I think this (holding water bottle) is symbolic, too . . . You offer something . . . It's very silly to say water, tea, or coffee is like a gift but anything you give . . . you don't need to do it. I went to my therapist for two years and

---

65. Bhabha, *Location of Culture*, 196.

she never gave me anything, you know? . . . It's just like an act of caring. Yeah, I just feel like you genuinely care. Yes, so that helps everything.[66]

When I started RDM, I reexamined every therapeutic framework I was taught in my clinical training. I did not want to blindly use the established framework that was set up by predominantly white Western psychoanalysts without truly understanding the reasons behind it.[67] Something as simple as offering water, tea, or coffee to clients, while seemingly unconventional, gives me a way of inviting clients into an anxiety-reducing environment. I also genuinely desire to offer them something to drink because I know from personal experience, the challenges of leaving my own therapy sessions parched. Being authentic in my movement toward freedom and empowerment has led me to empower others to do the same. Honest reflections and reclaiming my voice also included confronting harsh realities within me that had to be corrected.

Creating More Space

Confessions of a Colonized Colonizer

My inner work has revealed that I have unknowingly adopted colonial and sexist views of the white Western thinkers from my socialization as a child of missionaries. In my youth, I entered Southeast Asian countries as a lighter-skinned Korean child who came from a wealthier country. My father built churches, schools, and soup kitchens for the darker-skinned, poorer, indigenous people. I blindly accepted and followed a colonial perspective that has historically oppressed the countries in which we lived. I unconsciously thought that I must be better than the people around me because they needed our help. Without knowledge of the source or consequences of colonial exploits that spanned centuries, I shortsightedly and subconsciously viewed darker-skinned indigenous people as inferior. I

---

66. Ava, interview by author, July 5, 2017.

67. In a small private group conversation with Nancy McWilliams, the plenary presenter at the American Association of Pastoral Counselors (SE region) conference in Kanuga 2016, Nancy encouraged us to think beyond the framework that Sigmund Freud set up as his therapeutic frame. This framework has somehow been passed down as *the* frame that must be used in therapy, but she challenged this notion saying Freud created it for the people he was seeing in his context. Much has changed since then culturally, historically, and even in the field of psychotherapy itself.

recall condescendingly viewing the women who lived with us to provide domestic services for my family's home and mission center. Rather than as human beings, I only saw their roles. I separated myself physically and internally from the children who came to the school my father started by thinking that somehow I was smarter or better.

They also saw me and treated me in certain ways to curry my favor. I used their perception of me to justify the way I saw and treated them. In no way was I taught to reflect on how they really saw me and how I really saw them. In some ways, we were both flattening the other, trying to pull from the other what we needed, rather than being open for meaningful human relationships.

The painful realization of my own racist views and colonial sentiments years later led to acknowledgment of my wrongdoing, to deep repentance, and to a desire for change. How could I have been so blinded? Ignorant? Narrow-minded? Instead of appreciating and learning from the different voices around me, I participated in the silencing and devaluing of those I had come to see as "other." By dehumanizing the "other," I severed any chance I had for an authentic connection with my peers, thus preventing any growth and fellowship. By not seeing those around me as full human beings, I also rejected the sacred within them. This realization was made more excruciating because I knew what it felt like to be silenced and seen as the "other" by a dominating person or group.

I am aware that my own role as colonizer to others cannot be easily swept under the rug. It is a part of me that must be confronted. Feminist theorist bell hooks claims that if we "always seek to avoid confrontation, to always be 'safe,' we may never experience any revolutionary change, any transformation, individually or collectively."[68] A new space must be created that allows for confrontations both within oneself and with others as well as a space of empowerment to speak one's truth. Discord and conflict cannot be avoided but need to be worked through for true transformation. As I engage in creating this space within me, I extend this confrontation and empowerment to the clients of RDM. SGKAs need counselors who have the inner, mental space that opens to hold and empower as well as challenge their oppressive worldviews. By confronting my own faulty ideologies, and doing the hard work of self-critique, I am freeing up much-needed space to be available for my clients to occupy with their own stories, struggles, and transformations.

---

68. hooks, *Feminist Theory*, 66–67.

Opening the Red Door

Homecoming

Home Away from Home

Much of the strength and rootedness in my identity and role as pastoral caregiver comes from continued inner work. My longing for a home and belonging has led me to dig deeper into my spiritual and emotional roots. Family therapist Monica McGoldrick describes home as "a spiritual and psychological place of liberation. Home is a space, where we could all belong—with each other—strengthened by what we take from those who have come before us."[69] My years in the Th.D. program have been more than a rewarding intellectual journey. My studies have paralleled a homecoming where my voice and my sense of self have been safely welcomed. By studying the works of others who have powerfully expressed their voices, I have learned strategies to help my clients do the same. This process has given me permission to create a safety within myself for my voice to be heard. I have a home where I find belonging. At RDM, I am furnishing a home away from home with a distinctive style where others can also find belonging.

A deeper sense of rootedness came during a recent trip to Korea, the first time I have gone back in over thirteen years. Seeing my grandmothers and hearing the stories of ancestors long departed expanded my understanding of home and gave an added sense of rootedness. I discovered that I come from four generations of Christians on both sides of my family. My great grandparents embarked on a spiritual journey that goes back a century, the fruits of which are seen in my life. There are many pastors and caregivers[70] within my family tree, adding meaning and connection to my calling as pastoral counselor. I could see common themes of physical and emotional healing as well as God's generosity in the stories that I heard on this trip. As I made room in my heart for the faith stories of my ancestors, I felt more whole. Standing on South Korean soil, I could place myself in the flow of my family history. A renewed sense of peace and awe of the sacred added to this feeling of wholeness. I may have struggled with feelings of not belonging in the social locations and cultures of my lifetime, but within my family history, I identify with deep roots and find home. By traveling

---

69. McGoldrick. "Finding a Place," 102.

70. My maternal grandfather and uncle, my paternal great aunt and great uncle, and my father were/are all pastors, including my sister and brother-in-law. My maternal great grandfather and paternal uncle were/are elders of the church. Many of my aunts and cousins have careers in infant care and elderly care or in healthcare.

to South Korea, I figuratively and literally placed myself out of the socially constructed context of my daily realities and created a new place of belonging, a free space that allowed me to explore my roots and all the nuances that make up who I am. At RDM, I seek to take clients on a similar journey of recovering their spiritual and emotional roots to find new places of home and belonging.

Conclusion

As we have seen, RDM is comprised of multiple spaces. Postcolonial critique creates the space for the restoration of freedom and power that is necessary for all human beings. The physical space of RDM is created as a manifestation of Winnicott's potential space that holds the clients as they engage in transformative inner work. The mental and emotional space created by the counselor's own inner work is also crucial in what makes up RDM. As clients enter to embark on their own journey toward wholeness and home, the counselor's inner world must also be constantly evaluated.

How do the clients of RDM embark on their journeys that move them toward wholeness and finding home? Chapter 3 will examine the client's transformative journeys in RDM.

3

What Happens in Red Door Ministry

AS A KOREAN AMERICAN pastoral counselor working with SGKAs, I find it irresponsible to take Western theories in their entirety and apply them to the complex lives of SGKAs. Psychologists Song E. Lee and A. Valencia assert, "It is imperative that counselors understand how individuals shape themselves rather than trying to shape them into being healthy within a Western context."[1] One example of this can be seen in the different notions of self that SGKAs must navigate on a regular basis.

This chapter begins with the juxtaposition of Western and Eastern notions of self. This conflicting view of self often gives rise to a sense of shame. We will define shame through the views of Western and Eastern theologians and see how it connects to the lives of some SGKA clients in RDM. The shame seen in the clients' lives before their arrival to RDM presents concrete examples of this complex emotion. For the sake of clarity and deeper analysis, I will focus on the voices of Ava and Jason, two SGKAs of the four clients interviewed. Ava and Jason's experiences with shame prior to and during their time in RDM act as examples for the concepts and theories discussed. Psychological theorists D.W. Winnicott and C.G. Jung ground our analysis of what is helpful from Western theories in addressing shame. The voices of Korean American theologians Wonhee Anne Joh, Andrew Sung Park, and myself are considered to form a committee from which an alternative answer to Western theories is found. The chapter concludes with

1. Lee, *Multicultural Issues*, 59.

practical applications of how caregivers, therapeutic spaces, and pastoral care within a Christian context can engage in responsible intercultural care for those who live in both Western and Eastern spheres.

Western vs. Eastern View of Self

The Western notion of self emphasizes an individualism that stands apart or above the collective group. In *Moving Beyond Individualism in Pastoral Care and Counseling*, pastoral theologian Barbara McClure defines the term "individualism" in this way:

> [A] cultural ideology that prioritizes the individual as a center of moral value and fundamental philosophical construct; it also emphasizes the rights of the individual for freedom of thought and action . . . the individual is at the core of all epistemology and the formation of worldviews, as well as in formal valuation.[2]

McClure's perspective of the Western notion of self begins with the individual: all of the knowledge, values, and behaviors stem from the focus and advancement of self. In terms of mental and emotional health from a Western view, the individual strives for self-fulfillment, an end that finds satisfaction in interpersonal growth and integration. Although the Western individual self *is* connected to society through relationships, "the individual is prior to society and is the basic unit in society."[3] The Western individual is often socialized to put the self above the group or collective. The Western definition of health reflects the idea that the well-being of the individual often supersedes the welfare of the larger group.

The Eastern notion of self, however, stems from one's dynamic relationships and interactions with others. "The idea of American individualism is contrary to the Asian & Pacific Islander Americans values of individual sacrifice and collective and cooperative hierarchal family structures."[4] It does not make sense within an Eastern collective culture for a person to attempt to define herself apart from the larger group to which she belongs. This collective sensibility can be seen in the Korean understanding of the word "human." "The Korean term for human is *inn-gahn* . . . consist[ing] of two words, *inn* ("person") and *gahn* ("between"), denoting that a human being

---

2. McClure, *Moving Beyond Individualism*, 24–25.
3. Park, *Racial Conflict and Healing*, 72.
4. Lee, *Multicultural Issues*, 60.

exists between persons."⁵ With such emphasis on relationships and how one fits into a group, the Western values of independence and uniqueness are not as central to selfhood in the East. Instead, values such as harmony, balance, and relationships are vital for a well-functioning person in society.

The Korean word *woori* further explains this collective mindset. Korean American theologian Hee An Choi defines *woori* as "'a word that indicates the person himself/herself or several people who are on the same side.' It is a word that represents a person or the community to which a person belongs."⁶ *Woori* can be literally translated as "we," "our," or "us." The term, however, is also used to signify the possessive term "my" in the English language. Although there is a term that is the Korean equivalent to the English "my," Korean cultural usage of the term is extremely limited and *woori* is often used instead. This means that the Korean equivalent to "my house," "my family," or "my church" is "*Woori jeep* (house)," "*Woori gajoek* (family)," or "*Woori gyohwae* (church)." No one person can claim ownership to these units; they belong to the collective. Hearing a woman talk about her mother as "*Woori umma*" or "our mother" may sound strange to the Western ear but this is a cultural norm. Thus, the Eastern notion of self is deeply embedded in the relationship to the group. With no clear boundaries, the self cannot be separated from the system.

SGKAs are steeped in the Eastern values of group harmony that form the heavy pressures to succeed not purely for their own good but also for the honor of the family, community, and society. As seen in chapter 1, individual success becomes family success and parent success. In the Eastern perspective, acknowledgement and acceptance by the group requires conforming to group ideals. At the same time, the urge of Western individualism creates confusion and pain for SGKAs who attempt to define themselves as independent beings.

Shame

What results for those holding both Western and Eastern notions of self is a sense that they are simply, as many RDM clients say, "not good enough." With the complexity of living with both notions of self, forming a confident sense of self can be difficult. By not belonging fully in Western or Eastern culture, many SGKAs live on the margins, feeling "a sense of

---

5. Park, *Racial Conflict and Healing*, 75.
6. Choi, *Postcolonial Self*, 10.

persistent inferiority, worthlessness, abandonment, weakness, abjection, unwantedness, violation, defilement, stigmatization, unlovability and social exclusion . . . generat[ing] chronic shame."[7] Navigating the conflicting notions of self from both Western and Eastern perspectives can leave some SGKAs to see themselves as the problem. Most of the SGKA clients who enter RDM exhibit varying degrees of feeling "inferiority, worthlessness, abandonment, weakness, abjection, and unwantedness," illustrating their sense of shame.

Although all the clients came to RDM with different complaints and symptoms, the root cause of their diverse concerns is often shame. At a deeper level, all of them reveal thoughts of being inadequate and feelings of shame. They feel they cannot be accepted or loved until they are deemed worthy by fulfilling expectations set by their parents and community. The shame of not being worthy often leads them to silence their own voices and feelings. This muting of self can be seen in Ava through her feelings of "nonexisting"[8] and in Jason's intense feelings of "guilt, regrets, and shame."[9] These clients illustrate how shame can silence one's own voice and limit one's capability to live full lives of openness and creativity. When SGKAs are silenced, freedom is lost, safety is compromised, and a sense of home is jeopardized. To understand the destructive nature of shame, we must start with defining shame.

Shame and SGKAs

Defining Shame

Shame: Self-Deficiency

Pastoral theologian Donald Capps explores shame in his book *The Depleted Self*. He defines shame as the "response to our failure to live up to an ideal that we have held for ourselves . . . shame is therefore the experience of a self-deficiency."[10] This definition is especially relevant in this study of SGKAs who have been taught to meet the ideals of being a successful

---

7. Pattison, *Shame Theory*, 108.
8. Ava, interview by author, July 5, 2017.
9. Jason, interview by author, November 12, 2017.
10. Capps, *Depleted Self*, 72.

Korean American. For many SGKAs who do not feel that they measure up to these ideals, the result is often feelings of shame.

In *Shame, Theory, Therapy, Theology*, practical theologian Stephen Pattison presents shame as something that "encompasses the whole of ourselves; it generates a wish to hide, to disappear, or even to die."[11] Shame is not just a feeling of having failed; shame is tied to one's identity and how one views oneself; shame reflects what Pattison calls the "global self." Those living with shame have a "painfully diminished sense"[12] of self that is perpetuated by a "tacit internal monologue of self-criticism."[13] As we will see, both Ava and Jason show this constant internal monologue of self-criticism that leaves Ava apologetic for her existence and Jason frustrated at his numerous failures, threatening their hope and future possibilities.

Shame: A Threat to Hope

In *Agents of Hope*, Donald Capps identifies shame as a threat to hope. "Shame is the painful, after-the-fact realization that what was wanted did not happen, in spite of the fact that it was fully expected. Shame is also the painful discovery that the future image we projected was a misconception, a false or mistaken image."[14] This mistaken image of the future is often seen as a failure of self. Rather than looking to a variety of factors as to why "what was wanted did not happen," those who feel shame place blame for hope unfulfilled on the inadequacy and worthlessness of self.

By pointing to the self as the reason for failure of hope, many SGKAs can enter a place of hopelessness and feel stuck. "Shame, especially if it becomes chronic, is a threat to hope because it undermines the premise on which our hopes are based namely, our ability to anticipate what may happen and especially what is possible for *us*."[15] Future possibilities for change become hard to imagine as shame silences any voice of hope. Ava and Jason's hopes were threatened by their shame. Their self-critical monologue had drowned out any other voice from being heard. Dire desperation to get unstuck led Ava and Jason to RDM as a last resort.

---

11. Pattison, *Shame Theory*, 41.
12. Pattison, *Shame Theory*, 72.
13. Pattison, *Shame Theory*, 72.
14. Capps, *Agents of Hope*, 123.
15. Capps, *Agents of Hope*, 130–31.

Shame: The Result of Victimization

In *From Hurt to Healing*, theologian Andrew Sung Park categorizes shame into several groups.[16] We will focus on two, *humiliating shame* and the *shame of failure*, that are most relevant to the SKGA client's experience. "Humiliating shame arises as the keenly painful consciousness of something dishonorable, inappropriate, and outrageous done to a person by another."[17] The person is humiliated, which is a natural response to "an oppressive and unjust transgression"[18] that can lead the victims to "blame themselves for being helpless."[19] The injustice inflicted upon them is turned into shame as they perceive the reason for their humiliation as being their own fault.

Park's categorization of humiliating shame and the shame of failure is comparable to Pattison's description of chronic shame which he asserts as coming from "the experience of human individuals being [dishonored], disrespected or objectified . . . the individuals concerned have probably endured much that is difficult and destructive in their lives."[20] Many SGKAs have felt "dishonored, disrespected, or objectified" by their parents, by the Korean American community, and by American society as well. This kind of oppressive experience can have a destructive impact on their view of self because they also feel shame for being helpless to change the unjust systems in place.

The second shame Park unpacks is the shame of failure. This second shame comes from the failure to live up to the expectations of self and others. "As our ideal is unrealized, our ego turns that unfulfilled ideal into shame . . . burden[ing] us with the uncertainty of our ability to achieve a task."[21] This shame of failure recalls Capps' view of shame as a threat to hope. Both views throw doubt to our ability to accomplish possibilities. Park calls both humiliating shame and the shame of failure a "victim's shame" because both types of shame come from a harmful source, whether an offender or an expectation, that is forced upon the person.

---

16. His categories include 1) humiliating shame, 2)the shame of failure 3) the shame of discretion and 4) the shame of disgrace which other scholars would call guilt. Park, *From Hurt to Healing*, 37–44.

17. Park, *From Hurt to Healing*, 38.

18. Park, *From Hurt to Healing*, 39.

19. Park, *From Hurt to Healing*, 40.

20. Pattison, *Shame Theory*, 108.

21. Park, *From Hurt to Healing*, 41.

Shame and Guilt

Before we turn to Ava and Jason to illustrate these different views on shame, it is important to distinguish between shame and guilt. These two concepts are connected and often confused or substituted for the other. Capps differentiates the two: "Whereas guilt arises in experience from failing to meet the expectations, real or perceived, of others, shame is felt when the self has failed to attain its own goals, when this realization occurs that the self is incapable of achieving its ambitions."[22] *Guilt* is the feeling that comes from doing something wrong or failing others, whereas *shame* is the emotion that the entire self is inadequate. In shame, Pattison emphasizes that the "negative evaluation is on the entire self... [which] is painfully scrutinized and found lacking."[23] In short, "we *perform* guilty actions, but we *are* our shame."[24]

Park distinguishes shame and guilt in another way. He claims, "in general, shame emerges when one is helplessly wronged or hurt by others. Guilt arises when one commits sin or does not do right."[25] Park seems to separate the two by linking guilt with offenders and shame to those offended. It is interesting to note that for the Korean American theologian Park, the difference between these two concepts is seen in a relational context, whereas Western theologians Capps and Pattison locate both guilt and shame within the individual. Jason's experience with guilt and shame can help unpack the connection further.

Jason and Shame

Shame and Idealization

Jason describes where his internal self-critical voice stems: "Korean people are always judging each other and comparing themselves with each other ... there's so much focus on ... shame and what you didn't do ... there's no acceptance."[26] The constant judgment and comparisons from Korean parents and peers left Jason feeling he could never catch up and be accepted. The ideals of the Korean American dream and the push for attaining

---

22. Capps, *Depleted Self*, 34.
23. Pattison, *Shame Theory*, 126.
24. Capps, *Depleted Self*, 74.
25. Park, *From Hurt to Healing*, 35.
26. Jason, interview by author, July 15, 2017.

What Happens in Red Door Ministry

success (defined in chapter 1) left Jason with little room to explore and pursue his own desires and hopes for his life. Instead he was "dishonored, disrespected, or objectified"[27] by the people around him as one who needed to conform to the role of a good son or a successful Korean American man: both of which demand attaining high levels of education to ensure financial stability.

Many of these expectations also come from Jason's internalized ideals of being a man. His nine-year relationship with his girlfriend at the time added pressures on him to propose as men are expected to do in our society, but his lack of a steady income prevented him from doing so. In his family, he felt guilty that he could not take care of his mother financially as the good son, when "she basically [had] given her life up to give me the opportunities that I had."[28] He felt guilty for letting his loved ones down and not meeting their expectations. As his guilt increased with more actions and inactions he deemed wrong and unacceptable, Jason started to blame his "global self" as being lacking and deficient.

The failure to be an ideal version of the Korean American man filled Jason with shame. These "failures used to control me . . . it just paralyzed me"[29] as if they were "a physical handicap . . . I mean shit, it like broke me."[30] Jason's paralysis and brokenness came from the belief that these failures made him "unloved and unlovable. The self has a sense that it is defective and has a basic flaw that ensures its unacceptability and rejection by those whom it loves."[31] Jason not only felt others found him unacceptable and unlovable but also viewed himself in the same way.

In response to the external and internal negative judgments and comparisons that heightened his sense of shame, Jason started to hate the world around him. He hated those that placed these expectations on him. Above all, his shame led him to hate himself. He claims:

> My guilt, regrets, and shame became real because it disabled me. It broke me . . . My mind gained complete control over me. It's like taking a constant beating until your will is broken. I started hiding from others, from my friends, from my family. I started engaging in self destructive activit[ies]. I convinced myself I wasn't good

---

27. Pattison, *Shame Theory*, 209.
28. Jason, interview by author, July 15, 2017.
29. Jason, interview by author, July 15, 2017.
30. Jason, interview by author, November 12, 2017.
31. Pattison *Shame Theory*, 76.

enough, that I was useless and worthless . . . I was stuck in this constant cycle of self-destructive thought and activity.[32]

Self-destruction is a common response to a deeply embedded feeling of shame. "The attack self script is associated with feelings of disgust . . . about the self. The self cannot stand itself, rejecting itself as fundamentally disgusting, smelly and undesirable."[33] This "attack self script" completely silenced Jason's voice until "I couldn't speak for myself . . . my will was so broken, I had no will to do anything."[34] The failure to meet the idealizations had broken Jason's will to do anything. A specific script that dictated all his actions had replaced his true voice.

Shame and Gender Script

Mark Hearn claims, "society has created certain expectations of boys [and men] that are reinforced in their reoccurring performance. Society creates a gender script that projects acceptable behavior."[35] Jason felt that no matter how hard he tried, he could not live up to the gender and cultural script given to him. Jason's feelings of shame and failure would elicit strong anxiety for fear of experiencing more failures. He broke out in heavy sweat in any social or professional setting, preventing him from networking or completing interviews that would secure a job. This increased his shame of not being "man enough." Considering counseling or seeking any professional help also conflicted with this gender script. Jason explains, "I had too much pride 'as a man,' thought I didn't need help, thought I could fix things myself."[36]

Jason's shame "is closely associated with the wish to hide or to conceal oneself in the face of unbearable psychological pain."[37] This desire to hide can be linked to the concept of having too much "pride as a man." Jason's shame fueled the strong desire to hide behind the socially constructed mask of being "a man." To be open and honest about his shame and weaknesses would imply that he is not man enough to handle things on his own.

---

32. Jason, interview by author, November 12, 2017.
33. Pattison. *Shame Theory, Therapy, Theology*, 112.
34. Jason, interview by author, July 15, 2017.
35. Hearn. *Religious Experience*, 29.
36. Jason, interview by author, November 12, 2017.
37. Pattison, *Shame Theory*, 156.

What Happens in Red Door Ministry

As Jason's anxiety and self-destructive thoughts and activities increased, his desperation for change brought him to RDM. He realized he could no longer hide his pain and shame because they threatened to take away hope for any kind of future. As he confronted his idealizations and lay aside the male gender mask, Jason realized what he could and can continue to do differently:

> I wish I didn't like hold back . . . I still hide a lot behind like my past and it's still hard for me . . . so that people don't see or know who I really am . . . I hide behind the stupid shit I've done in my life or the bad things I've done, yeah, that's something I realize . . . I need to stop hiding.[38]

Jason is coming out of hiding his shame to enter places of freedom and hope. By learning more about himself, he is reclaiming his voice. Jason is accepting himself more as he challenges the idealizations of his gender and culture. His transformative journey will be explored in further detail with Western and Eastern theorists later in this chapter.

We now turn to Ava, who also started her journey from a place of shame.

Ava and Shame

Shame and Negative Emotions

Ava grew up in a home where expressions of negative emotion were not only frowned upon but were also seen as evidence of low worth. Her father often showed anger and violence when intoxicated and "my mother always talked bad about him so he was someone I didn't want to be like."[39] She received a clear message from an early age that any expression of anger reflected a defective self and made her unworthy of love. To cope, Ava avoided "bad" emotions because "every time I would feel like that, I thought there was something wrong with me. I'm a bad person for feeling like this."[40] She was shameful of feeling anger or any other emotion she labeled as "bad" and worked hard to suppress them. Unfortunately, this practice of silencing her "bad" emotions also closed the door on all emotions, leading her to feelings of "nonexisting."

---

38. Jason, interview by author, November 12, 2017.
39. Ava, interview by author, December 14, 2017.
40. Ava, interview by author, December 14, 2017.

Pattison claims that those who are unable to acknowledge their chronic shame often use other words to describe their experience. These are words "relating to the feeling of alienation, such as . . . estranged, deserted, rejected, rebuffed. Another set of words may relate to a sense of confusion—stunned, empty, lost, aloof."[41] These words are similar to the words Ava used to describe her condition before RDM: "I was just really deep in the feeling of nonexisting and I just felt like I didn't exist and those symptoms were getting worse and worse and I just felt desperate to feel something."[42] She described feeling estranged and alienated from herself and the world around her. There was also a sense of emptiness causing her to feel that she no longer existed.

This feeling of "nonexisting" came from the loud critical voices Ava internalized that "dishonored, disrespected, or objectified"[43] her. Her shame is a humiliating shame because she was not given permission to be fully human. She was taught from childhood that she cannot express the full range of human emotions. Bad emotions were deemed unacceptable and to have them made her entire self unacceptable. The monologue of self-criticism overshadowed her own voice and destroyed her sense of worth, leading her to constantly apologize for her existence. Ava explained, "I always say 'sorry' or I always feel bad . . . and so I *never* feel like I'm doing well. It's kind of like, I'm never happy with myself."[44] Upon further reflection, Ava exclaimed that this apologetic and self-demeaning attitude can be traced through the women in her family.

Shame and Gender Roles

Ava recalled her shock in seeing how her grandmother acted during a recent visit when she followed Korean gender roles:

> She's eighty years old . . . but serves everyone and does the ninety-degree bow to everyone . . . my mom told me something, it's like a Korean saying, like a woman is born a sinner or something like that . . . when I see or think about my grandma, that's exactly how

---

41. Pattison, *Shame Theory*, 157.
42. Ava, interview by author, July 15, 2017.
43. Pattison, *Shame Theory*, 209.
44. Ava, interview by author, July 15, 2017.

I think she lives, like always feeling like she has to make up for something that she's done.[45]

Ava's grandmother lives her life following the traditional Confucian ideal that a woman's life is to serve everyone around her. Grace J. Kim, further describes this Korean gender expectation:

> A woman was to obey her father while at home, her husband when married and her son if widowed. From Confucian cosmology came the notion that the female *yin* force, essential for harmony, ought to be passive and docile, following the lead of the more important male *yang* force.[46]

The harmony this yin and yang supposedly represented through these gender roles is a far cry from true equality and balance. The manifestation of this oppressive Confucian tradition in Ava's grandmother's ninety-degree bow elicited strong feelings of anger and shock in Ava as she began to see and to challenge the gender inequalities within the culture. Ava also realized that her mother continued this mindset of sacrificing her needs for the needs of others. In a painful and powerful moment in the interview, Ava admitted, "I'm doing the same thing, I'm saying the same things [to myself]."[47] It was as though being a woman in this culture and family meant women must live lives of atonement for their gender. They did so by placing others before themselves and apologizing for their existence.

Ava's shame is a family shame that had been passed down in the women of her family due to family and cultural norms:

> She is unlikely to be loved and appreciated for what she is in and of herself. She is likely to be required to act out some role in the family that helps that system to avoid confronting its shame, such as being . . . [a] good child (avoiding unwanted negative attention by adopting a conformist personality) . . . There will be no role models within the family whereby he or she can learn a sense of self-respect and more about his or her own boundaries. Shame is passed down the generations by the inevitable replication of family systems through unarticulated secrets, mysteries and myths over time.[48]

---

45. Ava, interview by author, July 15, 2017.
46. Kim, *Grace of Sophia*, 50.
47. Ava, interview by author, December 14, 2017.
48. Pattison, *Shame Theory*, 106.

By taking on the role of the good child, Ava worked hard to maintain the patterns of her family system. There was no love and support for Ava to be and to express herself. There was no role model in her family to show Ava self-respect and healthy boundaries. She silenced herself by telling herself, "'I don't want to be a burden,' so I'd rather just hold all this to myself than tell somebody."[49] Ava's sense of shame came from generations of women who were deemed unworthy and lacking.

As Ava questioned and challenged this destructive family and cultural tradition, strong feelings appeared to elicit change: "It makes me frustrated and super annoyed, seeing that, it seems like [mom] thinks that she has no power, or like no voice. And it's so much so, that she's used to it . . . she's just so used to asking, asking [for permission] . . . and for me that's frustrating. You don't need to do that, you don't have to be like that!"[50] Ava's work of going beyond shame is not just her own but is a pioneering journey that breaks generational patterns of shame. She is shedding the heavy coat of shame for the freedom to be unapologetically herself. Her transformative process is examined through several concepts from the Western psychologist D.W. Winnicott.

Western Psychological Theorists

D. W. Winnicott

Donald W. Winnicott (1896–1971) was a psychoanalytic theorist in the school of British Object Relations Theory, who mainly worked and derived his theories as a child analyst. Author of over twenty books and hundreds of papers, Winnicott left a deep impact on the Western understandings of a healthy self. Known for his creativity, playfulness, and unconventional approach to therapy,[51] Winnicott presented a unique interest in healthy human development as opposed to the emphasis on pathology that was more common for his time.

Winnicott wrote extensively on the relationship between caregiver (focusing on mothers) and child as well as the necessity of a trusting

---

49. Ava, interview by author, July 5, 2017.

50. Ava, interview by author, July 5, 2017.

51. Winnicott used creative activities such as the squiggle and the spatula to assess and treat his young clients. These involved drawing and playing with props with another person that revealed the nature of a child's relationship with herself as well as the world around her. Sollod and Monte, *Beneath the Mask*: 237–40.

environment for healthy selves to develop. He was also interested in examining the in-between space between fantasy and reality, which he addressed in his concepts of *transitional phenomena* and *play*. Winnicott believed that the successful navigation of this space nurtures the development of a *true self*. His work has been invaluable in the formulation of how a safe and trusting environment can lead to the development of a more free, flexible, and creative individual. Winnicott's theory on creativity and transitional spaces provides useful perspectives in the care of SGKAs in RDM. The flexibility and movement between inner and outer realities depicted in his theories reflect the flexibility and movement needed to move RDM clients beyond shame. The three concepts we will explore from Winnicott's theory that connects with Ava's transformative work in RDM are *transitional object/phenomena, play,* and *true self*. We begin with his best-known concept of transitional object.

Transitional Object and Transitional Phenomena

In his paper "Transitional Objects and Transitional Phenomena," Winnicott defines *transitional objects* and *transitional phenomena* as the "designation of the intermediate area of experience, between"[52] a "me" and "not-me"[53] object. In other words, he is describing a use of an *object* in the child's process of separating herself from the mother/caregiver. Objects such as a "blanket, teddy bear, or doll—that belong at once to [the child] and to the outside world,"[54] act as placeholders that bridge the inner illusions and outer realities of the child. A transitional object is the "first not-me possession"[55] that helps the child learn to distinguish themselves from outside objects, such as the child's mother. This separation from the mother allows the child to establish a real relationship with the mother. This separation is the transition the child makes from thinking that the mother (especially her breasts) is the result of magical thinking that the child herself has created out of her desire to feed, to seeing the mother as a "not-me," a separate object who exists in the real world and caters to the child's needs. This transitional phenomenon allows the child to build

---

52. Winnicott, "Transitional Objects," 2–3.
53. Winnicott, "Transitional Objects," 3.
54. Rudnytsky, *Transitional Objects and Potential Spaces*, xii.
55. Sollod and Monte, *Beneath the Mask*, 255.

trust with her mother when a good-enough environment is primed for the development of a healthy individual.

The transitional object itself "becomes vitally important to the infant for use at the time of going to sleep and is a [defense] against anxiety."[56] The object can soothe the child when she feels anxious about the process of separation and transition. The transitional object also shows the growing agency and power of the child. Winnicott claimed that seven special qualities are present in the relationship between the transitional object and the child. Four of them are:

- The child assumes rights over the object.
- [The object] is affectionately cuddled as well as excitedly loved and mutilated.
- [The object] must never be changed unless changed by the infant.
- [The object] must survive instinctual loving and also hating.[57]

These four qualities show the child exercising freedom of feeling, thought, and action. The function of transitional objects and the process of the transitional phenomena provide clues as to how SGKAs can separate themselves from the "mother" of shame as they distinguish their behaviors and feelings from their sense of worth and value.

Transitional Objects and Shame

Transitional objects can help shamed people transition from identifying their entire selves as bad to separating out their negative feelings from their "global" selves. This distinction can lead to a healthier, more authentic relationship with themselves as well as with the people around them. Stephen Pattison reminds us that:

> Shamed people often feel that they experience a kind of negative inner voice that makes unrelenting disparaging and critical comments about the self. This inner voice, which represents a fantasy bond with the 'good,' [idealized] but persecutory inner parent, must be confronted and changed.[58]

---

56. Winnicott, "Transitional Objects," 5.
57. Winnicott, "Transitional Objects," 7.
58. Pattison, *Shame Theory*, 164–65.

Winnicott's concept of transitional phenomena provides us with possible paths that could bring people out of a place of shame. With the help of transitional spaces and objects, clients like Ava can confront the persecutory inner parent, or the "mother" in Winnicott's term, as a "not-me" possession. The breaking of a "fantasy bond with the 'good'" idealization is analogous to the transitional phenomena of moving between "the subjective hallucination and objective reality testing."[59] These confrontations and changes give agency to the formerly shamed as a relationship of trust and safety allow for their voices to be heard.

Ava's Transitional Object

As I discussed in chapter 2, RDM and the counselor can act as transitional object for SGKA clients who are forming their own voices and strengthening their sense of self. For Ava, her weekly sessions with me have soothed her anxieties as would any transitional object in the process of confronting and distinguishing herself from the negative self-judgmental voices within her. The therapeutic hour has come to be "an intermediate area of experience"[60] as she transitions from the internal illusions that heightened her shame to the objective reality of acknowledging her existence and value. She has separated herself from the "mother" of conformity and found agency and value in expressing her emotions, whether she had previously labeled them good or bad. She is "just allowing myself to be me."[61]

Ava expresses her affection and love for the transitional object of RDM and the counselor by uninhibitedly saying, "you just feel like a friend . . . I really like you (laughter)."[62] Ava has also mentioned several times in our sessions that she carries around an "inner Jinny" with whom she holds internal conversations. This "inner Jinny" helps her feel less anxious while simultaneously challenging her to lower the volume of self-criticism. Ava is playing with an important transitional object when she turns to this voice in her head that she calls" inner Jinny."

---

59. Sollod and Monte, *Beneath the Mask*, 256.
60. Winnicott, "Transitional Objects," 3.
61. Winnicott, "Transitional Objects," 3
62. Winnicott, "Transitional Objects," 3

Opening the Red Door

Play and True Self

In his 1967 paper "The Location of Cultural Experience," Winnicott defined *play* as "neither a matter of inner psychic reality nor a matter of external reality," [63] but as something that resides "at the point in time and space of the initiation of their (child and mother) state of separateness."[64] Reminiscent of his concept of transitional phenomena, play is located neither in the inner psychic reality nor the external reality but occurs in a "third area."[65] Creativity and imagination are required to take inner fantasies and bring them into the external world. Playing in this third area of potential space between mother and baby (counselor and client) serves as the grounds from which a healthy self blooms.

Winnicott further described play in the following way:

> *It is play that is universal* (his emphasis) and that belongs to health: playing facilitates growth and therefore health; playing leads into group relationships; playing can be a form of communication in psychotherapy; and lastly, psychoanalysis has been developed as a highly specialized form of playing in the service of communication with oneself and others.[66]

Play requires a flexibility and openness to the other person with whom one is playing. This communal exchange is key not just for play but also for the building of trust between parent (Winnicott's "mother") and child or one between a client and counselor.

In fact, Winnicott described psychotherapy itself as play. "Psychotherapy has to do with two people playing together . . . the therapist is directed toward bringing the patient from a state of not being able to play into a state of being able to play."[67] A certain kind of environment is needed to bring someone from a state of not being able to play to a place of imaginative creativity. In the playground of potential space, the client feels "relaxation that belongs to trust and to acceptance of the professional reliability of the therapeutic setting."[68]

---

63. Winnicott, "Location of Cultural Experience," 129.
64. Winnicott, "Location of Cultural Experience," 130.
65. Winnicott, "Location of Cultural Experience," 138.
66. Winnicott, "Playing: Theoretical," 56.
67. Winnicott, "Playing: Theoretical," 51.
68. Winnicott, "Playing: Creative," 74.

According to Winnicott, the first experience of a trusting, safe, third space was in the relationship between a mother and baby where play emerges as the tool to form a basis for a *true self*.[69] The true self is defined as "real, spontaneous, and creative... At core, True Self is a synonym for the 'experience of aliveness.'"[70] When the baby or client takes the sum of their experience from playing in a trusted, safe environment, a sense of true self with all its potentials of authenticity, spontaneity, and creativity emerges. Winnicott proclaimed, "In playing, and perhaps only in playing, the child or adult is free to be creative and use the whole personality, and it is only in being creative that the individual discovers the self."[71] The experiences of play in a trusted and safe environment allow the true self to surface.

Play and True Self and Shame

The "wish to hide, to disappear, or even to die"[72] that shame generates hinders play and the development of the true self. Shame inhibits play because it "undermines our disposition to trust that the world is as we believe it to be."[73] Moving beyond shame demands trust to be built in a third space where the person can, with creativity and imagination, nudge their true self to come forward.

The building of trust between the client and the counselor is vital for combating shame. According to Pattison, "This is likely to be difficult. Chronically shamed people are inherently mistrustful of human relationships and of exposing themselves to others."[74] By modeling acceptance and relational consistency within the therapeutic frame, the client slowly learns to trust and play with the counselor. The emboldened client can leave behind their defenses against anxiety and their true selves can lead them to an "experience of aliveness."

---

69. Winnicott, "Playing: Creative," 75.
70. Sollod and Monte, *Beneath the Mask*, 254.
71. Winnicott, "Playing: Creative," 73.
72. Pattison, *Shame Theory*, 41.
73. Capps, *Depleted Self*, 78.
74. Pattison, *Shame Theory*, 167.

Opening the Red Door

Ava's Play and True Self

A trusting and safe environment helped Ava move from a place of "unaliveness . . . reached by an extreme of regression"[75] to feeling truly alive. "I feel like I don't have to hide things, won't have to feel embarrassed or shame or whatever, not judged."[76] Much of this trust and acceptance came from a decision I made to share some of my own stories with Ava. Carefully choosing what, when, and how to share, I entered into this potential space with her as *my* true self, inviting her to join me in the play of psychotherapy. Ava shared her experience of my transparency. "You talk about youself, and not all the time, but the few times that you do, for me that means a lot . . . So, when you share something about your family or like your past experience in something, it helps me be more comfortable to share things and trust you."[77]

Having built trust and acceptance between us, Ava has come to see RDM as a potential space where I, the counselor, am on her side, encouraging her true self to manifest. Even when I appear confrontational in some of my responses or in asking what she calls "slicing" questions, Ava does not doubt the safety and dependability of the third area we have created together: "I think at this point I know your intentions, I know you mean well for me. Because that is like, already set, I don't think like with any of the questions you mean any harm by it."[78]

Ava explains this transition through the concept of giving permission. "I feel like you gave me the ultimate permission to give myself permission (laugh). No, . . . you helped me understand that I can give myself permission."[79] Seen through Winnicott's theories, Ava is giving herself permission to play, to explore, to engage in a trusting relationship, and ultimately to be her true self. Her true self helps her feel "real, spontaneous and creative." As Ava puts it, our time together "helps me be me."[80]

Winnicott's theories on transitional object/phenomena, play, and true self provide one framework for Ava's transformative work. Her "magic[al]" journey from feelings of "nonexisting" to giving herself

---

75. Winnicott, *Human Nature*, 132.
76. Ava, interview by author, July 5, 2017.
77. Ava, interview by author, July 5, 2017.
78. Ava, interview by author, December 14, 2017.
79. Ava, interview by author, July 5, 2017.
80. Ava, interview by author, December 14, 2017.

permission to fully be herself serves as a Winnicottian example of how a healthy self can develop.

Jason's journey from "guilt, regret, and shame" to freedom and acceptance will now be discussed using the theories of Carl Gustav Jung.

C. G. Jung

Carl G. Jung (1875–1961) was a Swiss psychoanalyst and a protégé of Sigmund Freud who eventually broke away from Freud's circle to form his own theory of the human psyche. Jung's work was uniquely creative and spiritual compared to some of the other Western theorists of the field. He used art, dance, and other artistic media not only in his work with clients but also in his personal exploration of self. In over twenty books written and edited during his lifetime and the publications of his writings and drawings posthumously, Jung argued for investigating the self that may remain untapped in the individual psyche[81] and the collective unconscious.[82]

Much of Jung's theory appealed to an intuitive, nonlinear way of defining and seeing the human psyche. He opened the door for a more creative and artistic way of integrating the many conflicting and tension-filled parts that reside in every individual. His call for wholeness and acceptance of our full selves, including those parts we deem negative, is particularly appropriate in our divided, conflict-filled world today. For SGKA clients, the use of a creative medium allows them to tap into and express their inner worlds that words, steeped in cultural meanings, make inaccessible. I will explore three of Jung's ideas and analyze how they pertain to confronting shame: the concepts of *self-exploration, individuation,* and *shadow* provide the structure for examining Jason's transformation in RDM.

Self-Exploration and Individuation

In 1957 Jung wrote *The Undiscovered Self,* claiming that "Man [sic] is an enigma to himself."[83] He called for individuals to embark in *self-exploration* and free themselves from the constraints of society's expectations. Jung

---

81. Psyche is defined as the sum total of all the conscious and unconscious contents of the mind. Sollod and Monte. *Beneath the Mask,* 160.

82. Transpersonal unconscious built from the experience of a collective human history. Sollod and Monte. *Beneath the Mask,* 147–76.

83. Jung, *Undiscovered Self,* 45.

believed that health came from finding the answer to who one is, in the acceptance and discovery of self, in all its complexities. "The meaning of my existence is that life had addressed a question to me. Or conversely, I myself am a question which is addressed to the world, and I must communicate my answer, for otherwise I am dependent upon the world's answer."[84] Jung grieved the fact that many individuals have been dictated to by society rather than these individuals having an influence on it. This being dictated to rather than having influence leads to a large range of inner turmoil and despair as we either strive to fulfill external standards or struggle against the oppressive forces that limit or take away our power and agency. Following societal pressures can make us lose sight of our sense of purpose and meaning in our lives. Many SGKAs daily face these oppressive societal pressures that come from living double lives.

In self-exploration, individuals become their own person apart from family and societal expectation. Jung called this *individuation,* a process of "becoming an individual being . . . our innermost, final, incomparable uniqueness, becoming one's own self."[85] Jung explained his own individuation as "[a]n affirmation of things as they are: an unconditional 'yes' to that which is, without subjective protests—acceptance of the conditions of existence as I see them and understand them, acceptance of my own nature, as I happen to be."[86] Through self-exploration and individuation, the individual shows a "willing[ness] to fulfill the demands of rigorous self-examination and self-knowledge . . . deeming himself worthy of serious attention and sympathetic interest."[87]

Self-Exploration and Individuation and Shame

The self-diminishing nature of shame may delude an individual into thinking that other matters take precedence over the quest for self-exploration and individualization. For many SGKAs, the stressors of heavy cultural pressures to succeed add to the challenge of making time and space for self-examination. The biggest hindrance to self-exploration and individuation for the shamed person, however, seems to be fear. Shame's effects are to "make us more fearful, less willing to take risks, and more concerned for

84. Jung, *Memories, Dreams, Reflections,* 318.
85. Jacobi, *Psychology of Jung,* 100–101.
86. Jung, *Memories, Dreams, Reflections,* 297.
87. Jung, *Undiscovered Self,* 89.

self-survival than for self-expansion and new experiences."[88] Jung's concepts of self-exploration and individuation give us a way to face this fear of self-expansion.

Andrew Park's second category of shame, the *shame of failure*, also reflects this fear: "We hesitate before we venture out because of our past shameful experience of failure. Such shame eats up our courage to risk."[89] Clients confronting shame must gain the courage to venture out from society's demands and their own constricted view of self. In the liberating space of RDM, room is made for deeper self-exploration and individuation as clients reclaim their value and worth, even experience an exhilarating sense of liberation such as Jason found in his journey.

Jason's Self-Exploration and Individuation

RDM served as a gateway for Jason's self-exploration and individuation: "I learned a lot about myself. It was the first experience . . . I ever had of truly learning about myself and like, and it was kind of a shock . . . how little I knew about myself."[90] As Jason discovered himself and solidified his sense of self, he also came to a place of self-acceptance. He boldly proclaimed, "It's ok to be myself, it's ok to struggle, it's ok! It's ok to feel a certain way."[91] His sessions in RDM helped Jason give himself permission to be. "It lets me be who I am . . . it helped me be ok with who I am. It really shattered the image of what I thought I was supposed to be. Or what I thought every[one] else wanted me to be."[92] Jason's path to self-exploration and individuation parallels Jung's description of his own process: "I had the overwhelming impression of having just emerged from a dense cloud. I knew all at once: now I am *myself!* . . . at that moment *I came upon myself.*"[93]

This self-acceptance led Jason to a place of unbridled freedom as he took off the heavy burdens of societal pressures that he had carried for all his life:

---

88. Capps, *Depleted Self*, 79.
89. Park, *From Hurt to Healing*, 41–42.
90. Jason, interview by author, July 15, 2017.
91. Jason, interview by author, July 15, 2017.
92. Jason, interview by author, July 15, 2017.
93. Jung, *Memories, Dreams, Reflections*, 32.

> [My time at RDM] gave me freedom . . . Freedom is really important to me because the happiest times in my life, the most fun times in my life . . . are the times when I feel free . . . it's the times when I feel liberated . . . When the things you think are important don't matter, where people's opinions don't matter.[94]

Jason found happiness, fun, and freedom in his self-exploration. This sense of freedom empowered Jason to face all aspects of himself, including the imperfections and flaws he previously worked so hard to ignore.

Shadow

Jung called what some might call the darker side of our psyche the *shadow*: "To become conscious of [the shadow] involves recognizing the dark aspects of the personality as present and real. This act is the essential condition for any kind of self-knowledge."[95] One of the first stages of individuation and self-exploration is the recognition of our shadow and the acknowledgement of our imperfections. Humility and courage are required for anyone to face their shadow and imperfections. Without the recognition of our shadow, we are quick to see ourselves as good and moral and:

> convince ourselves and the world that it is only *they* (i.e., our opponents) who are wrong. It would be much more to the point for us to make a serious attempt to recognize our own shadow and its nefarious doings. If we could see our shadow (the dark side of our nature), we should be immune to any moral and mental infection and insinuation.[96]

Jung claimed we must face the conflicts and hidden shadow within us not purely for our own growth and development but to also strengthen our relationships and to handle the dangers and shadows of our times. "Recognition of the shadow . . . leads to the modesty we need in order to acknowledge imperfection. And it is just this conscious recognition and consideration that are needed whenever a human relationship is to be established."[97] The awareness and acceptance of our shadow lead not only

---

94. Jason, interview by author, July 15, 2017.
95. Jung, *Psyche and Symbol*, 8.
96. Jung, *Man and His Symbols*, 73.
97. Jung, *Undiscovered Self*, 101.

to a harmonious and balanced view of self but also to harmonious and balanced relationships.

Awareness and acceptance must also include the positive sides of us. Jung observed, "it is not merely the 'shadow' side of our personalities that we overlook, disregard, and repress. We may also do the same to our positive qualities."[98] Our shame strengthens when we "overlook, disregard, and repress" our positive side to focus too much on our shadow side. What Jung ultimately argued is the embrace and development of all aspects of our personality that lead to wholeness.

Shadow and Shame

Jung's concept of shadow depicts that the mere acknowledgment and acceptance of the negative loosens its powerful grip on us. In the same way, "shame must be acknowledged and owned if it is to be healed. Without insight and knowledge into the nature of shame a person will be unable to get rid of, or dissipate it."[99] The safety, trust, and space of RDM encourage clients to muster up the courage to face and accept their full selves, including the shadow and the positive sides. This self-acceptance is a vital step in combating shame. "[A]ccepting oneself unconditionally in such a way that one regards oneself as neither more nor less than an imperfect, fallible human being"[100] brings healing and self-love.

Jason's Shadow

Much of the pain Jason felt prior to his time in RDM came from the constant self-criticism and self-dismissal that fed his demons of guilt and shame. He could not be liberated until he faced and acknowledged what he called his "failures and weaknesses." Most of the work Jason engaged in during the counseling process was to face and acknowledge his shadow. He shared that his work in RDM "just made all those things real and tangible and it made me come face-to-face with it . . . It helped me fight or like, be able to work through them . . . It was no longer abstract."[101] By dealing with them

---

98. Jung, *Man and His Symbols*, 51.
99. Pattison, *Shame Theory*, 166.
100. Pattison, *Shame Theory*, 164.
101. Jason, interview by author, July 15, 2017.

honestly and openly, Jason created new ways of viewing himself. "Instead of just having it all in my head all the time, or just shoving it on the side or burying it deep down," he started to acknowledge and accept his demons, guilt, and weaknesses as a part of himself.

Interesting to note is that as Jason embraced his shadow side, he slowly started to see the good within him as well. Jason's feelings of being inadequate blinded him from seeing his strengths and good characteristics. The acceptance of his shadow side helped him see himself more clearly. Jason was reminded of his compassion for others and his desire to help and connect with the people around him and that this mattered more than meeting the expectations of success and idealizations: "It helped me realize . . . the things that I always thought were important in life, like being there for people, or trying to make people happy, or loving people or accepting people." His own self-acceptance increased his ability to love and accept those he previously hated.

Winnicott and Jung in Red Door Ministry

As Ava and Jason show us, a trusting, accepting environment can create a potential space where clients can engage in the play of self-exploration. By diving deeper into themselves, these clients found not only a measure of self-acceptance that eased the pain of their initial complaints, but they also reclaimed their voices as unique, valuable individuals. They found the freedom to live with more confidence and joy through their process of individuation. Taking off the burdens of societal pressures, they carved out their own paths toward who they want to become through their creativity and imagination. This empowerment and agency gave each of these clients the motivation and energy to continue their journey toward wholeness and home.

I am aware that my exploration of Winnicott and Jung is incomplete. I do not attempt to cover their theories in their entirety because they do not fully reflect the experiences of Ava and Jason. This leads to the question of how we can use theories created from a different time and cultural context in an ever-changing intercultural setting.

Gaps in Western Theory for Second-Generation Korean Americans

Western psychological theories push toward individuation. Counselors who situate themselves in the Western notion of self suggest to their clients the importance of creating firm boundaries. These counselors might suggest "moving out" to help a client separate from what they see as an unhealthy enmeshed relationship with members of a group so the client can form a stronger sense of self. For example, when I was dealing with boundary issues with my own mother after my father's death, my Western oriented therapist suggested exactly that. She repeatedly asked what was hindering a grown woman like me, at the time in my late 20s, from leaving my mother and carving out my own space, both internally and externally, that would free me from what she viewed as a fused,[102] unhealthy, and overly stressed relationship. It was difficult for me to explain the strong cultural pull that makes such a decision seem selfish and disrespectful. I felt my counselor did not understand the tension of sitting in both Western and Eastern concepts of self.

Concepts such as Jung's self-exploration appeal to the Western notions of self but do not leave much leeway for the Eastern understanding. From the Eastern perspective, the goals and process of reaching Jung's definition of individuation can sound selfish and self-absorbed. Even Winnicott's attention on creativity and play can be viewed as ways of disturbing the group's harmony and important traditions, social hierarchies, and structures.

What other theories must be considered to give voice to the experiences of SGKAs? Is it acceptable to pull various threads from Western theories to weave something that fits the needs of this unique population? Or does one need to start from Eastern thought and philosophy? Another question emerges: where does one find Eastern theories of psychology?

Eastern Theorists

The theories of psychology and the practice of psychotherapy are relatively newer disciplines that trace their roots back only a century.[103] These theo-

---

102. Murray Bowen's concept of fusion describes a low level of differentiation where "in the closeness of an intense relationship the emotional selves of each blend or fuse together into a common self, a 'we-ness.'" Papero, *Bowen Family Systems Theory*, 51.

103. Although philosophers, theologians, writers and historians have been trying to understand human nature from ancient times, it was not until the 1900s with the work of Sigmund Freud that the field of modern psychology began to take shape. Sollod and

ries originated in the West and depended on a view of self and a definition of health that are Western. Thus, finding Eastern psychological theories which do not draw from Western theories is difficult. Because of this, I turn to Korean American theologians for concepts to address the shame many SGKA clients feel. With respect to the Eastern emphasis on the collective, a theory will be formulated by turning to a committee of contributors. Wonhee Anne Joh's concept of *jeong*, Andrew Sung Park's concept of *hahn*, and my metaphor of a *fusion chef* will work together to form a Korean-American answer to the Western theories of Winnicott and Jung.

Wonhee Anne Joh

Wonhee Anne Joh is a Korean American theologian who uses feminist and postcolonial theory in the formation of an Asian American theology. Joh uses the concept of *jeong* with postcolonial concepts such as hybridity and mimicry to reframe a *Christology* that reflect the abject experiences of Korean and other Asian Americans. We will use her definition of *jeong* to see how it can confront the shame felt by many SGKAs.

Jeong

Often translated as "love" in English, Joh uses the Korean word *jeong* as the way of being in relationship with the diverse groups of people who make up our communities. Her appeal for *jeong* starts with the recognition of the dehumanizing, violent experiences Korean Americans have of racism as well as sexism for the Korean American women living in the United States. She challenges Korean Americans and other Asian Americans to view and connect with American society through the messiness of *jeong*.

Joh distinguishes *jeong* from love saying, "*Jeong* is more powerful, lasting, and transformative than love. *Jeong* makes relationship 'sticky' but also recognizes the complex and dynamic nature of all relationalism."[104] *Jeong* keeps us in relationship with one another even when we hurt and fail each other because it "recognizes not only the dignity and worth of oneself but also that of others."[105]

Monte, *Beneath the Mask*, ix.

104. Joh, "Violence and Asian American," 146.

105. Joh, *Heart of the Cross*, 147.

She further defines *jeong* as a:

> Korean way of conceiving an often complex constellation of relationality of the self with the other that is deeply associated with compassion, love, vulnerability, and acceptance of heterogeneity as essential to life. It not only smooths harsh feelings, such as dislike or even hate, but has a way of making relationships richly complex by moving away from binary, oppositional perception of reality, such as oppressor and oppressed. I argue that *jeong* is the power embodied in redemptive relationships [106]

By embracing "compassion, love, vulnerability, and acceptance of heterogeneity as essential to life," we recognize our connection and interdependence with the larger world. "[W]hether we want to admit it or not, [we are] always connected to one another . . . *Jeong* recognizes that we are indebted to others."[107] Unlike Western concepts, *jeong* emphasizes our entangled connections and relationships we cannot be without.

Jeong allows us to relate to one another as full, richly complex human beings. "*Jeong* is such space that does not erase differences between cultures but rather recognizes difference while creatively undermining biases."[108] Rather than labeling differences as the *other*, something foreign and abnormal, *jeong* dismantles these prejudices to open space for full relationships. It pierces through the negation and abjection many SGKAs have internalized as shame.

Jeong and Shame

Many SGKAs have had the degrading experiences of being rejected as full human beings and also being treated as what Joh calls an abject. "The abject is understood as that which the self sees as the unclean, foreign, and improper."[109] Living double lives and feeling homeless in both cultures can lead SGKAs to internalize being "unclean, foreign, and improper." The result of such abjection is shame. Joh's concept of *jeong* helps the previously shamed to reclaim their dignity and worth through choosing to be in relationship and standing in solidarity with others who have similar

---

106. Joh, *Heart of the Cross*, xxi.
107. Joh, "Violence and Asian American," 147.
108. Joh, *Heart of the Cross*, 40.
109. Joh, "Violence and Asian American," 150.

dehumanizing experiences. "Choosing to live by and through *jeong* is to claim one's agency and power in a situation of powerlessness."[110]

The relational nature of *jeong* ensures that the agency and power claimed go beyond the individual to become the agency and power for the group. *Jeong* embraces the group rather than distinguishing an individual from it:

> Whenever the communal is emphasized and honored, I have found the presence of *jeong* . . . Lack of *jeong* is most noticeable in cultures that have adopted capitalist, individualist notions of the self and the violent projections necessary to sustain this sense of self in opposition to the other.[111]

Jeong is a powerful force that can bring not only individuals beyond their shame but also the entire community. It confronts and challenges the internal "self-critical monologue" within the individual as well as the oppressive biases within societal systems and cultural perspectives.

Jason's Jeong

As Jason combated his negative, self-judgmental inner voice, he used his awareness and *jeong* for others to help them do the same. "I remember every week after I saw you, I would take what I did in there and pass it on to my friends."[112] His relationships remained intact while he confronted his shame. He was not content to go alone in this journey toward freedom and joy. He wanted to share his happiness from his transformation with others around him. "I'm happy now, and I feel like I bring a lot of energy to other people too. I like having fun and I try to share that with others because it's not fun alone . . . the freedom leads to my happiness and I dunno, it's contagious, I guess."[113] In fact, Jason sometimes writes updates of his life and sends them to a large group of people through email. At the end of every email he writes a paragraph inviting his friends to RDM so that they can embark on their own transformative journeys. Several clients have acted in response to Jason's vulnerable and powerful plea and have come to RDM for their own transformative work.

110. Joh, "Violence and Asian American," 147.
111. Joh, "Violence and Asian American," 156–57.
112. Jason, interview by author, July 15, 2017.
113. Jason, interview by author, July 15, 2017.

What Happens in Red Door Ministry

Ava's Jeong

Ava exhibited deep *jeong* in her awareness and response to other people's shame and unjust experiences. During the interview she talked about her elevated sensitivity to "something wrong" in people and circumstances around her:

> I'm very good at . . . telling if something is wrong . . . being able to tell, especially if it's an emotional thing, or like depression or something like that, I've been able to pinpoint those kind of people out and, umm, I think it's gotten better, my ability to do that . . . And because I'm second generation, I've always been aware, and especially because of how I grew up, in a very, very White dominant [environment], you know, I was one of two Asians in school . . . there was a lot of injustices. Umm, but I guess, I have, I dunno, I feel like I have more power to do something about things [now].[114]

Ava used her heightened awareness of injustice and others' mental and emotional concerns to approach them and show them *jeong*. Her self-understanding and self-acceptance had fueled a desire to understand and accept others. Her reclaiming of her voice gave Ava the power to address the abjection around her. She was able to use her identity as a SGKA as an advantage. Ava encourages other SGKAs to "use the fact that you're a second generation . . . [to] bring about change . . . If you do something, that will be a ripple effect or something. Just believe whatever you do will create change."[115] Through *jeong* Ava shows how far she has come from shame and abjection. Like Jason, she is not content to experience this change on her own but wants to motivate her friends and the SGKA community to join her. This desire for unity and oneness in this journey is reflected in Andrew Park's concept of *hahn*.

Andrew Park

Andrew Sung Park takes the painful transitions of immigration and the wounds of racism the Korean American community experience as the starting point of his theology. He uses the Korean word *han* to describe these deep pains. Park suggests new ways of seeing the oppressors and the oppressed, claiming both need salvation and liberation. He takes orthodox

---

114. Ava, interview by author, July 5, 2017.
115. Ava, interview by author, July 5, 2017.

theological concepts such as sin, forgiveness, and holiness, among many others, as well as Korean concepts such as *hahn* (oneness), *jung* (sticky love), and *mut* (balanced beauty), to reformulate a theology that is relevant for the lived experiences of Korean American Christians. We will focus on one concept, *hahn,* to examine how it can address shame.

Hahn

Hahn (not to be confused with *han*–deep woundedness) is a complex concept that denotes several characteristics. First, *hahn* is used to signify "the divine, pointing to greatness, sublimity, immensity, brightness, honor, ultimacy, infinity, majesty, and magnificence."[116] The Korean word for God, *hahn-u-nim,* attests to this meaning. The word also indicates "*Oneness.* It indicates a circle that has no beginning and no end."[117] This oneness is symbolic of wholeness that takes us beyond binary thinking. The last meaning of *hahn* is one of:

> *paradoxical inclusiveness*, pointing to an indeterminate boundary. It embraces one and many, and whole and part, simultaneously . . . the radical openness of *Hahn* emphasizes tolerance, acceptance, and creativity in spite of difference and lack of accord. *Tolerance* is passive inclusion, *acceptance* is active embracing, and creativity is the dynamic interaction between ying and yang.[118]

These various meanings of *hahn* come together to present a sense of a majestic, divine wholeness that embraces the one and the many where differences are not diffused but celebrated as balanced and creative parts of a large oneness to which we all belong. As opposed to the Western notions of individualization and distinction from the collective, *hahn* attempts to include and accept the one and many as well as the similar and different in its embrace. This notion of *hahn* can serve as a powerful tool for SGKAs in facing shame.

---

116. Park, *Racial Conflict and Healing*, 108.
117. Park, *Racial Conflict and Healing*, 108.
118. Park, *Racial Conflict and Healing*, 108.

What Happens in Red Door Ministry
Hahn and Shame

Hahn integrates, accepts, and points to greatness and wholeness, while shame hides, alienates, and depletes the self. *Hahn's* added dimension of divine greatness overshadows any feelings of self-deficiency that come from the shame of failing an ideal. *Hahn* can help SGKAs to transcend from the isolated, divided, and shameful self to the embrace of "the openness of life ... to attend every person [including themselves] as the divine."[119] *Hahn* encourages tolerance and acceptance of the uncertainties, differences, and the multiple.

Ava's Hahn

Ava's journey in RDM reflects *hahn* as her self-understanding and acceptance boasts not only her confidence and self-esteem but also her desire to accept and embrace the people around her. She is learning to value her voice as coming from God. "I just feel like I'm here to love people. I think that's my calling. Like, whether it's just you know young women who I feel God has really pulled me toward or you know just people in general. And I can't do that if I'm not healthy."[120] Ava practices this "paradoxical inclusiveness" toward people because she is able to see them as belonging to the oneness of humanity, all of whom having worth and value despite of or perhaps because of our differences.

Ava starts this inclusive embrace with her own sense of self. "[Before,] I'd be very mean to myself, but once things make sense, when I see things ... I give myself some more mercy, like leniency ... I'm just more accepting and nicer to myself."[121] As she moves away from shame to embrace the multiple cultural formations and various aspects within her and in others, *hahn* allows Ava to face the ambiguities and varieties in one majestic embrace.

Jason's Hahn

When asked to describe what RDM felt like, Jason exclaimed, "that room makes me think of like a cloud, I'm sitting on a cloud or something like

---

119. Park, *Racial Conflict and Healing*, 115.
120. Ava, interview by author, July 5, 2017.
121. Ava, interview by author, July 5, 2017.

that, something . . . [that] makes me think of heaven."[122] Thus, began a journey that would remind Jason of the divine light and magnificence that lies within him and that unfolds in his life. His heavy shame was lifted as he entered the uplifting embrace of *hahn* that he found in RDM. The freedom and joy he uncovered results from *hahn*, the radical embrace of self and others he had failed to do before. As *hahn* moved Jason to wholeness, he wanted others, still struggling with living a divided double life, to also live in "paradoxical inclusiveness."

For Jason, the division is most apparent in Korean Americans. "I think Korean Americans need therapy more than any other people . . . because I feel like we are the most divided people. Like, even when we're together there's division."[123] He explained that the division is both "within ourselves, like, internally . . . [as well as externally] in like, all those church splits."[124] Park's concept of *hahn* can bring divine oneness and openness to differences in individuals and to the collective in their movement away from shame. This openness to life can lead to new life and new creations as the multiple threads of influences, thoughts, and cultures come together in fusion.

My Approach

Wonhee Anne Joh's *jeong* and Andrew Sung Park's *hahn* point to an openness and connectedness to the opposing and different factors that often keep groups separate. Their call to accept and stay in relationship with those different from us requires vulnerability and creative new ways of relating to the other. *Jeong* and *hahn*, however, do not "go the distance" in explaining how such differences can bring us to the destination of the new, let alone describe what the new looks like. I propose the metaphor of a *fusion chef* to describe how differences might be brought together and how something new can be formed to nourish a diverse world away from shame into places of freedom and agency.

---

122. Jason, interview by author, July 15, 2017.
123. Jason, interview by author, November 12, 2017.
124. Jason, interview by author, November 12, 2017.

What Happens in Red Door Ministry

Fusion Chef

The *fusion chef* metaphor has helped me navigate the uncharted waters of pastoral counseling for SGKAs. As *fusion chefs*, both the caregiver and client come together with knowledge and experience of various cultures that must be integrated in an inventive way to create something new, healing, and empowering. Each caregiver, client, and community is composed of various cultural, socioeconomic, historic, racial, and gender dimensions. There are no two people or communities that are the same. Many SGKAs, as well as the larger general population, live between cultures and in places of uncertainty and ambiguity. Grace Ji-sun Kim talks about the potentials of such in-between places:

> At first glance it may be a place of undesirableness but however more, it may also be a place of providence as it provides room to become creative and insightful, where the imagination of the mind can release powerful images of survival and sustenance. It can be in this hybrid place where salvation can be found and experienced.[125]

This hybrid place is where the fusion takes place. Like a chef who forms exciting new dishes by turning to different cultures and traditions to serve the ever-growing culturally savvy consumer, the *fusion chefs* who are giving and receiving care draw from the different cultures and viewpoints around them to address the negative aspects of shame and build toward wholeness and freedom. Each depends on their own creativity and resourcefulness to offer what is needed in whatever context they find themselves. Using one method, theory, or perspective in giving and receiving care is not only obsolete and irrelevant but also irresponsible and incomplete.

Although there is large progression from the monocultural history of the field of pastoral care and counseling, I question whether cultural competency, which often stops with the exposure to and knowledge of a different cultural context, is enough for giving and receiving care today. Like Joh's *jeong* and Park's *hahn*, is openness toward others enough? If we return to the *fusion chef* metaphor, cultural competency and openness can be seen as a chef who has knowledge of other cultural cuisines but who is also someone who mainly stays within one tradition or method in their cooking. A *fusion chef* does not stop with the knowledge of a different cultural cuisine, rather she takes the essence of that culture and the essence

---

125. Kim, *Holy Spirit, Chi*, 84.

of another to combine them fashioning a new creation that people from a mixed cultural background can appreciate and enjoy. Simply being open to the *other* is not enough; we must be willing to enter their lives and culture.

As individual intercultural pastoral counselors, caregivers, and clients and as collective groups, communities, and society, we can take the wisdom and values of one culture and bring it to another culture, creating a hybridization that creatively addresses the needs of our diverse cultural contexts. The outcome we can hope for is a movement toward wholeness that can be characterized by freedom and joy as we witness clients and communities reclaiming their voices and living in *jeong* and *hahn* amid various cultures. The new "dish" created from combining and honoring these differences can nourish, sustain, and strengthen the individual and the collective to live as authentic, courageous people in a polarized world. We can move beyond the binary and act as human bridges who close the gap between various groups.

Fusion Chef and Shame

The shame of not being "good enough" exhibited by many of the SGKAs who come to RDM comes from feeling ashamed of their differences and otherness from the rest of the group. Not fully belonging to either the Korean or American culture, some SGKAs try to downplay the one or the other, depending on where they find themselves, to fit in to the larger group. The metaphor of the *fusion chef* encourages SGKAs to see their differences as unique and invaluable ingredients rather than being reasons for their shame. Their hybridity can be the starting point for powerful, new integrations for their complex intercultural identity as well as for the intercultural issues of our world. This concept of hybridity is further developed in chapter 4 as we look at how SGKAs can create new centers from the margins.

By bringing in both cultures into the conversation of forming the new, SGKAs can be the guides who help other Korean Americans, and all other Americans, to enter into relationship and community with each other. SGKAs are uniquely positioned to bring first-generation Koreans into the larger American society as well as to welcome other Americans to enter Korean American culture and communities. By doing so, SGKAs can create rich, fulfilling interactions and connections that lead to the healing and growth of all involved.

What Happens in Red Door Ministry

Ava and the Fusion Chef

My work with Ava provides an example of this *fusion chef* metaphor at work. We had to navigate through the Korean and American sides of Ava that encompassed both the Western and Eastern views of self and health. The relief of her negative symptoms and personal growth was intricately tied to her desire to see her family move closer to mental and emotional health as well. Her progress did not feel complete without the rest of her group joining in the journey.

For example, as patriarchal norms and notions of sacrifice were questioned in RDM, Ava took her new awareness home to her family. She saw the cultural gender roles and shame that continued to chain her mother to feel obligated to act in destructive, self-sacrificing ways. Ava hoped to help her mother start on a similar path toward self-value, self-acceptance, and freedom. Ava's concern became more urgent as she saw her mother's physical and emotional health deteriorate. At the same time, Ava continued to feel overwhelmed by her mother's lack of boundaries when she demanded that Ava solve and address many of her mother's day-to-day obligations such as dealing with bills and traffic violations. Ava was torn because she felt a deep connection and obligation to her mother and her mother's well-being while also wanting to maintain her own sense of self apart from her mother.

As *fusion chefs*, Ava and I gathered the various ingredients of cultural norms and philosophical concepts from both cultures. Ava could resonate with the values of individuation and often dreamt of leaving home and carving her own path. On the other hand, Ava's *jeong* and connection to her mother elicited a need to stay and help with finances and daily tasks. We wrestled with how Ava could feel satisfied given these two seemingly opposing viewpoints. Ava realized that she could strengthen and enforce certain boundaries to ensure her own self-care within a shared space. We discussed how Ava could create her own space, both physical and metaphorical, while she cared for and invested in her mother's financial, emotional, and physical health. Ava named spaces and times at home or in her car where she could find solace and center herself without outside distractions or obligations. Since the time that this *fusion dish* was implemented over a year ago, Ava has returned to the same issue. The decision to stay and care for her mother was satisfactory at the time, but Ava now found herself in a different place with additional perspectives. We are now gathering newer ingredients for another possibility. The work of a *fusion chef* is never simple or finished but requires continued learning and practice to create a new dish that meets the needs of different, ever-changing individuals and communities.

Jason and the Fusion Chef

In Jason's case, his path to freedom and empowerment was fused from a strong leaning toward a more Western view of self. As he came out of a place of shame, Jason decided to move to a new state and begin a new chapter that was away from the high expectations of the Korean American community. His Eastern notion of self, seen in his strong connection to his mother, elicited feelings of guilt with which he struggled initially: "I didn't want to leave my mom, for sure, and she definitely made me feel guilty for leaving . . . [but] it was the need to take care of myself . . . the desperation to fix my life and worry about me and take care of me and do something for myself."[126] Jason's need to separate himself and create his own life was stronger than the pull to stay with his mother. We discussed the opposing forces within him before he left. After examining each of the ingredients from different cultures within him, Jason concluded that the path that most closely resembled following his inner voice was the one that told him to risk a new adventure in a new state. In an interview months later, Jason boldly affirmed his decision: "I moved to [new state] and it brought me to the biggest turning point in my life. You don't understand how happy I am living here . . . It's a dream come true."[127] The *jeong* for his mother and the Korean American community he left behind remains, as does the mindset of *hahn* which keeps the door to his heart and vulnerability open. Upon considering all the various cultural pulls, as well as his emboldened voice, starting anew in a new state and community has allowed Jason to live in freedom and wholeness.

Neither Ava's nor Jason's experience exemplifies a general standard of care that addresses the complex cultural formation of SGKAs. The image of *fusion chef* can act as a guide for the diverse clients of RDM as they create their own *fusion dish* that is the most relevant and satisfying for their journey toward health and growth. Although there may not be definitive, formulaic answers to the questions of engaging in effective intercultural care for SGKAs, as co-chef in the kitchen, I am constantly learning to take on each person's cultural situation with the utmost respect, humility, and

126. Jason, interview by author, July 15, 2017.
127. Jason, interview by author, July 15, 2017.

openness. With the *jeong* and *hahn* that bind us together, the clients and I continue to creatively work and play together as *fusion chefs* to discover potential ways to address their unique intercultural locations.

Beyond Shame

The Red Door Ministry Model in the Therapist and Therapeutic Environment

Far too many therapists and counseling centers are stuck in Western methods or perspectives in caring for their intercultural clients. Theory and practice centered around a Western notion of self and health dismisses the hybridity of cultures that exists in SGKAs and other intercultural populations. There has been a push for therapists, pastoral counselors, and other caregivers to be culturally competent in their ways of care, but how? Through education, self-critique, and immersion in various cultures, I propose a method of care that addresses the whole person.

The Caregiver

Educating oneself about different cultures through books, movies, and in conversations can help a caregiver learn the diverse ways that cultures see the self, define health, and understand human nature. Many caregivers go no further and claim cultural competency from their exposure to the literature available or from having new knowledge of a different culture. Without self-critique to allow this new knowledge to personally challenge, stretch, and question one's own biases and prejudices, no real change can be expected. The additional step of immersion into a different culture pushes a caregiver to the exciting, sacred space of true transformation, for both the caregiver and whomever the caregiver encounters. *Jeong* and *hahn* keep the caregiver in relationship even in the midst of conflict and tension that arises from confronting and valuing differences. The caregiver must become a *fusion chef* who goes beyond learning the recipe of different cultures to entering into the kitchen to cook new dishes that reflect one's constant growth from their continued education, self-critique, and immersion.

Opening the Red Door

Therapeutic Environment

The caregiver must bring this ongoing personal growth and transformation into the therapeutic environment. Education comes from allowing the client to teach their own culture without imposing what the caregiver assumes she knows. By remaining open to learning about the client's experience of negative symptoms, shame, and their complex culture, the caregiver can critique the theories and methods available, evaluating them for relevancy and usefulness. As the therapeutic relationship strengthens, the caregiver immerses herself into the client's life and allows the relationship to impact her practice and life just as the process changes the client's life. All of this is held together within a strong therapeutic frame that guarantees safety for vulnerability, openness, and courage. In terms of the *fusion chef*, the caregiver invites the client to be a co-chef so they can work together to create a nourishing "dish" that renews, heals, and leads to wholeness.

The Red Door Ministry Model in the Therapeutic Environment of Christian Churches

Although chapter 3 has focused on the transformations of Ava and Jason during their therapeutic process, the location of RDM within a Korean American church extends its possible influence into the larger church. By offering workshops and other opportunities for diverse groups within a church, usually divided by generational, cultural, and language gaps, to gather together, communal shame and other concerns can be addressed. Education for parents about having healthier boundaries can help them to lessen the pressure some have for their children to meet certain expectations so the chronic shame of failure can be avoided. Opportunities to share meals and talk about family narratives and personal stories of struggle and hardships in a formal or informal way can encourage a mindset of *hahn* and a heart of *jeong* for all who are gathered. First, 1.5, and second generations must be given a space to immerse into each other's lives and worldviews without bias or harsh judgement.

    Scripture must be reframed to ensure that it is not being used as a shaming tool for the community. As Grace Kim declares, "the ultimate norm by which the Scriptures are judged is whether they are oppressive or liberative."[128] Korean American Christians must learn to read scripture

---

128. Kim, *Grace of Sophia*, 21.

with a critical eye, interpreting it with the understanding of its complex cultural contexts and problems. Rather than trying to cover up any contradictions or issues, they must immerse themselves into the tension and conflicts, avoiding an easy, generalized, set belief system that could do more harm than good.

The metaphor of the *fusion chef* can be used within the Korean American church context as churches allow for curiosity to lead them to be open, to learn, and to use new skills and techniques to make more nourishing and enjoyable creations for the whole community. In this metaphor, the *fusion chef* is not the one who changes the ingredients. The Holy Spirit is the heat and fire that transforms the ingredients into a dish that feeds and nourishes the soul. The *fusion chef* simply brings the important ingredients together and allows for the space, time, and heat to make transformation possible. Likewise, the caregiver or pastor or church is not the one that heals, but rather the one that creates the space where important boundaries and opportunities are given for God to bring about new life. Chapter 4 looks further into the work of the triune God in the empowering transformations happening in RDM.

4

Transformations in Red Door Ministry
Theological Implications

EVEN NEAR DEATH'S DOOR, my father's active playfulness and deep affection for us remained untouched. I'll never forget his timeless words: "What I want to do most right now is to play music and dance with all of you!" We all laughed, and I said, "One day, daddy, we'll do it one day." That was an especially poignant statement because I had rarely seen him dance in all the years that I was blessed to know him. Even at the last days of his life, my father managed to create a beautiful, lively, and dynamic image and we were all invited to take part in it. In my eulogy, a couple of days later, I shared this moment with those who had gathered to grieve and to celebrate my father's life: "He's in heaven now where the angels are playing majestic music and he's dancing with God and all the saints who have gone before us and *one day* we will all join him and dance together in the warm embrace of our Heavenly Father."

My personal growth and work at RDM have helped me see that joining the dance with God is not something that happens only in heaven but is an open invitation that God extends in our daily moments. Every day is an opportunity to join the divine activity of renewal, growth, and transformation. The image of the divine dance remains a powerful guide in my personal and professional understanding of self, God, and others. In this chapter, the image of the divine dance also serves as a powerful metaphor that can guide our considerations for the dynamic transformations seen in the lives of RDM clients.

Pastoral Theology

This practice of taking lived experiences and engaging in theological reflection serves as the foundation for pastoral theology. In "Contemporary Pastoral Theology: A Wider Vision for the Practice of Love," pastoral theologian Nancy Ramsay traces the field's development from its focus on the "clinical paradigm's concern for individuals ... [to the] wider public horizon for care."[1] In the past few decades, pastoral theologians have recognized that the development of human beings does not occur in isolation but in relationships and systems where key issues of "justice and truthfulness and a value for human rights"[2] also need to be considered.

Thus, Emmanuel Lartey defines pastoral theology as the "critical, interpretive, constructive and expressive reflection on the caring activities of God and human communities."[3] This chapter will engage in pastoral theology as experiences of the four RDM clients are critically, interpretatively, constructively, and expressively reflected upon in relation to their social locations on the margins of their communities. God's active role in the care of these SGKA clients will also become apparent throughout the chapter.

Red Door Ministry Six Step Transformation Model: From Margins to New Centers

To look at the theological and psychological movements the four RDM clients make from being on the margins to creating new centers, this chapter will outline and explore the steps of the dance the clients take when they accept God's invitation to partner in the divine activity of transformations and new possibilities. These steps are explained through both social and theological concepts from the works of various theorists as well as through the RDM clients' voices. Because each client's dance with God continues to develop, proclaiming a conclusive number of steps from start to finish is difficult. I can, however, outline the steps I have seen the clients take so far, leaving open the possibilities for subsequent steps. I have charted the clients' transformative process in six steps. These steps have taken them from living in shame on the margins to becoming empowered co-creators, with God, of new centers. The steps are:

1. Ramsay, "Contemporary Pastoral Theology," 157.
2. Ramsay, "Contemporary Pastoral Theology," 160.
3. Lartey, *Pastoral Theology in Intercultural*, 14.

1. Opening and embracing possibilities
2. Identifying oppressive systems
3. Identifying redemptive elements
4. Using redemptive elements to challenge oppressive systems
5. Owning power and agency
6. Co-creating new centers

Step 1: Opening and Embracing Possibilities

We begin discussion of the first step RDM clients take by examining the traditional use of the dance metaphor. The dance is seen as an activity that creates room for possible growth and change.

The Divine Dance

The metaphor of dance has long traditional Western roots in the explanation of the triune God. Theologians throughout the centuries have turned to the image of a divine dance to describe *perichoresis,* an understanding of the different parts of the trinity. This "mutual interpenetration of the persons . . . indwelling each other in a 'mutual interiority'"[4] depicts the three dynamic parts of one God. The image of dance is often used to show the interplay of God's oneness and the three persons of God in movement.

Pastoral theologian Paul Fiddes encourages participation within this dance for both a deeper understanding of God and for a partnering with God in the divine movement. By becoming partners in the divine dance, we can step in line with God's will as God steps into our lives. Fiddes concludes his interpretation of the dance metaphor with these words: "The drama of the human life can only take place within the greater drama of the divine life. Our dance relationships can only happen within the patterns of the larger Dance."[5] By joining in the larger, ultimate Dance of God, we become more open to new relationships, opportunities, and growth as space is created for new possibilities. The invitation to dance with God gives

---

4. Fiddes, *Participating in God,* 47.
5. Fiddes, *Participating in God,* 184.

SGKA clients a hopeful and empowering metaphor that opens the door for powerful transformations.

The Invitation to Dance and Embracing Possibilities in Red Door Ministry

Clients of RDM enter a space where room is made by the Holy Spirit to work in revealing new insights and fostering change. A client's first steps through the door of RDM are already a "yes" to the Holy Spirit's invitation to the divine dance: a movement toward freedom, empowerment, and new life. God's invitation, however, is often not as obvious to the clients who enter RDM. Many claim an urgency or desperation for change as reasons for coming. As a pastoral counselor who has witnessed many new clients enter RDM, I must conclude that these feelings of urgency and desperation are in fact God's invitation to step into a dance to move toward new life.

Both Ava and Jason claimed desperation as the reason for their arrival at RDM. Ava remembered: "I just I felt like there was no other option and so I was just like kind of desperate."[6] Jason echoed Ava's sentiments saying, "I knew that if I didn't go I'd be in trouble."[7] Later in the interview Jason stated, "I realized that God's been speaking to me my entire life,"[8] and starting his journey at RDM was a response to this speaking. These clients' openness and their desire to change pointed to a softening of their hearts and a flexibility of their perspectives that may have been created by their experiences of living on the margins as SGKAs. Straddling different cultures, their tentative positions in both worlds may indicate a larger willingness to join in the divine dance that invited them to create their own centers. The divine dance became the container through which RDM clients could move from marginal existence to central living.

Rose gave a different explanation as to what brought her to start her journey in RDM:

> I felt like my heart needed something, like I needed to, umm, take care of something . . . I had been talking to people about counseling for a while now because the church that I go to, umm, they talk about it all the time and they like recommend people to go all the time . . . I felt like it was the right time.[9]

6. Ava, interview by author, July 5, 2017.
7. Jason, interview by author, July 15, 2017.
8. Jason, interview by author, July 15, 2017.
9. Rose, interview by author, July 6, 2017.

Although God's invitation was not explicitly mentioned in her interview, Rose clearly felt her need to take care of "something" in her heart at this particular time in her life. The thought of coming to counseling had already been planted by her conversations with other people at church. Her decision to come to RDM was a bold "yes" to the invitation to partner with God for much-needed change in her life.

Dancing at Red Door Ministry

The therapeutic hour itself often feels like a free-style dance session. Both clients and I remain open to addressing whatever themes or topics the Holy Spirit may bring up within our time together. Although God is often not openly mentioned by name within the sessions, I am aware and open to the promptings from God's spirit as I sit across from clients. There are very few sessions with set agendas in RDM. Most are open-ended sessions that allow for creativity and the possibility of taking us to unforeseen places of healing and insights. The back-and-forth movement of questions and answers, the ebb and flow of sitting in respectful silence and in passionate declarations, and the building of trust in the relationship all reflect aspects of the dance that occur in RDM. As the four clients joined in the dance, they started to identify the oppressive systems that push them onto the margins, limiting their freedom and power.

Step 2: Identifying Oppressive Systems

Margins

Accepting God's invitation to be a dance partner began with the clients' recognition of where they initially stood in society. By living on the margins of American society and the Korean American community, many SGKAs have been pushed to the side of the dance floor and may find that they have been left standing at the proverbial "edge of the room." They are often prevented by oppressive systems from freely dancing or moving to the center of the room. Before unpacking more of the effects of such marginal existence, we must first define margins.

In "Who's on Whose Margins?" Australian cultural researcher Michael Hurley analyzes the concepts of margin and center. First, he defines marginality as:

Transformations in Red Door Ministry

- The sets of social relations that are indicative of structures of social, political and/or economic inequality and/or disadvantages; and
- The cultures of the people who are affected by these structures.[10]

Hurley then examines why and how people are marginalized. He suggests that belonging to a group that is smaller in number, not having full economic, social, or legal access as equal citizens, and having a negative social image[11] may result in one's acquiring a marginal status. He also claims that defining marginality in comparison to the center is complicated. Claiming the metaphor of margins and center as an "unequal distribution of power: a powerful [center] and a less powerful margin"[12] oversimplifies the relationship between the two. In fact, margins cannot exist without the center and vice versa. The diffused line and complex interwoven relationship between margins and center require deeper thought. This discussion will be further examined in step 4.

Being Marginalized

Hurley admits that his analysis of margins and centers falls short in addressing how marginality feels and impacts individuals and groups. Being on the margins points to feelings of being excluded from the center. Wonhee Anne Joh suggests that "[m]arginality . . . is best understood as a nexus, the matrix where two or more worlds are interconnected yet none is central. Thus, to be in between two worlds, Asian and American, for example, means to be fully in neither."[13] SGKA clients are familiar with these feelings of being excluded from the center, yet connected to both from the margins.

SGKAs who feel marginalized by white and non-white people may also have a "sense of personal threat to safety"[14] and can become hyper-vigilant as seen in the cases of anxiety, depression, and other mental health concerns expressed at RDM. Some SGKAs have also internalized their feelings of marginality as shame (assessed in chapter 3).

As they entered the divine dance in RDM, the clients started identifying the oppressive systems and voices that felt threatening if the clients

10. Hurley, "Who's on Whose Margins," 172.
11. Hurley, "Who's on Whose Margins," 170.
12. Hurley, "Who's on Whose Margins," 178.
13. Joh, *Heart of the Cross*, 64.
14. Hurley, "Who's on Whose Margins," 180.

failed to conform to the system's standards. All of the clients interviewed showed a degree of devaluing of self and of ignoring their needs as they pushed themselves to preserve and yield to the central "norms" that oppressed them.

Rose's Feelings of Marginalization

Rose shared these feelings:

> I find myself very anxious when things are not done efficiently or when people are holding me back from reaching my goal . . . I think that there's something in my mind that says that if I can be productive, then I can be successful, and if I'm successful, then ultimately, I will be loved.[15]

Without high performance and productivity, Rose felt she would not be loved, not be seen, and not be acknowledged. This constant struggle to prove her worth and attain approval "when people are holding me back" came from Rose's feelings of marginality. In our time together, Rose identified her family and the Korean American church as spaces where she felt most marginalized. To confront these oppressive structures, she felt the need to prove her value through high performance and productivity. Rose felt tired and dejected from being placed on the margins and constantly trying to prove to others and to herself that she was worthy of being seen and heard. Although Rose felt marginalized by external oppressive systems, Sam exhibited an internalization of oppressive voices.

Sam's Feelings of Marginalization

Sam showed caution and self-consciousness in the way he acted with others. He was careful to act in certain ways that he thought others would see as acceptable behavior, conforming to a strict standard he created for himself. Sam did this by limiting his interactions and holding back from authentically expressing himself. He lacked confidence because he was afraid that if he did not act in certain ways, he would be rejected. Sam felt threatened by the pains of rejection and worked hard to fall in line with acceptable, oppressive systems of thoughts and behaviors. This constricted version of self stemmed from having been marginalized by his social relations:

---

15. Rose, interview by author, December 1, 2017.

> A lot of that comes from acknowledgment and acceptance and, umm, I always thought that acknowledgment and acceptance came out of worth and you know not, not being able to perform or being able to be in a certain level. Uh, you know I felt like I often had to pretend or do certain things or say certain things so that I would have that acceptance and I would have that acknowledgment.[16]

Sam acted out of fear that he would not be acknowledged or seen as "of worth" unless he thought and acted in ways that were acceptable to centralized social structures. Although Sam did not clearly explain the details of what these acceptable standards of behavior and speech were, his feelings of marginalization and restrictions from his social relationships were undeniable.

Both Rose and Sam depicted a devaluing of their own self-worth and a muting of their authentic voices as they turned to oppressive social structures as judges of their worth. Identifying the oppressive systems and the pain they had inflicted had a healing effect on these clients as they moved to the next step of reframing and reclaiming their marginality as places of strength.

Step 3: Identifying Redemptive Elements

Turning the Margins into Places of Possibilities

SGKAs' existence and worldview are valuable and necessary because of their unique position to expand the center and reach other groups on the margins. Joh explores the exceptional assets of marginalized people: "The paradox for many marginalized people is unique: because one exists at the boundaries, one is able to bring a creative convergence to the dialectics of traditional thinking between object/subject, Western/Eastern, female/male, creature/"non"-creature, earth/cosmos, spirit/body, roots/routes, margin/center."[17] Those on the margins have the most potential for creative thinking and action because of their ability to embrace and be in the midst of the tension of seemingly opposing forces. They have been "socialized to see always more than their own point of view,"[18] giving them a wider perspective and appreciation for the nuances and experiences of others that those in the center may miss.

---

16. Sam, interview by author, November 18, 2017.
17. Joh, *Heart of the Cross*, 2.
18. Joh, *Heart of the Cross*, 61.

Social activist and scholar bell hooks further explains this transcendent worldview from the margins:

> Living as we did—on the edge—we developed a particular way of seeing reality. We looked both from the outside in and from the inside out. We focused our attention on the center as well as the margins. We understood both . . . We were a necessary, vital part of that whole.[19]

SGKAs and other marginalized groups are in incredibly important positions to see the center with critical eyes and to introduce what God wills for the whole world. They can see from the outside (margins) who and what is happening on the inside (center) as well as to see from the perspectives of the inside (center) who and what is happening on the outside (margins). Prophetic voices from the margins have spoken messages of hope, love, freedom, justice, and equality changing the flow of history. By seeing the value and potentials of being on the margins, marginalized groups can find new meaning and divine purpose in their lives.

New Ways of Seeing

As RDM clients have stepped into this redemptive third step of the divine dance, they have claimed new ways of seeing God and of seeing themselves through God's eyes. These revelations have been a powerful force that moves the clients to remarkable transformations. Andrew Park claims: "Our *seeing* is as crucial as God's revelation. Without our *seeing*, God's revelation is not revelation to us . . . Inseparable from God's revelation, *seeing* is the key to bringing salvation and liberation to creation."[20] Clients of RDM exhibited *seeing God's revelations* in their journeys at RDM.

One of the first insights the clients showed was the recognition of their own value and position on the margins. Park continues: "Too often, the oppressed, do not appreciate [them]selves because of [their] damaged self-image. As long as [they] do not appreciate [them]selves, [they] neither have the ability to heal [them]selves nor do [they] know how to appreciate others."[21] RDM clients have taken off the colonized lens that contributed to their viewing themselves as lower than white people.

---

19. hooks, *Feminist Theory*, xvi.
20. Park, *Racial Conflict and Healing*, 130. His emphasis.
21. Park, *Racial Conflict and Healing*, 152.

Rose mentioned: "[SGKAs] have this like white superior complex, where they imagine that whites just have this superiority around, above everyone, but like, that's not true."[22] Other SGKAs and marginalized populations must examine themselves carefully and pull out any racist and sexist roots that might damage their self-image so that they can reclaim their worth and significance from God's perspective.

Finding New Sight at Red Door Ministry

Rose's Step Toward Redemption

Rose found affirmation from God that moved her toward self-acceptance and valuing her worth. Rose's progress in her emotional health was closely linked with important theological insights. Her realization of how God viewed her moved Rose from wanting to be free from all negative emotions, especially anxiety, to integrating and learning to process them in a healthier way. In her interview, Rose shared:

> So I realized that God was not asking for me to change like who I am but he [sic] was asking me to like to step into the freedom of who I am. Not to just abandon my natural instincts and my natural emotions, my compassion for people and who I am, . . . but he's [sic] actually asking me to step into freedom . . . And like be ok with it . . . he's [sic] like "accept who you are and don't, don't just imagine . . . or don't just put who you are aside because you think this is what I want from you. I created you the way I created you because I wanted you to be this way." And if my heavenly father says that I should be this way, shouldn't I step into it a little bit more deeply?[23]

Once Rose started to understand God's acceptance of her and God's desire for her to live in freedom, she began to let go of the harsh oppressive standards from those around her as well as those she placed within herself. Although Rose grew up hearing about God's love and acceptance, she commented: "I don't think I fully understood because I kept on thinking I need[ed] to change myself . . . I just thought healthy meant 'not me.'"[24]

---

22. Rose, interview by author, July 6, 2017.
23. Rose, interview by author, July 6, 2017.
24. Rose, interview by author, July 6, 2017.

As she responded to God's invitation to live and dance in freedom, Rose started to see her negative emotions not as something to be ignored and avoided at all cost but as important parts of her that relayed messages of who she is and what is important to her. These negative feelings came from being marginalized for most of her life, and they helped her to reclaim her value and identity. Out of the anger, pain, fear, and anxiety she had previously avoided, Rose found the strength to stand up for herself and claim who she is as worthy. As she sank more deeply into God's love and freedom, she no longer needed to prove her worth to God or to others because God already had claimed her as worthy. Rose explained: "I give myself room to breathe and not use God as like a way to be productive, but a way to just be and relax."[25]

Participating in God's movement in her life and seeing herself through God's eyes was helpful for Rose to face the fears that have risen from being marginalized. As her understanding of God's love and acceptance grew larger, her fears of rejection shrank. Rose learned to embrace how God created her and found new places of rest. Her understanding of self in relationship with God became an important factor in her emotional health. Her dance with God in this step redeemed what she previously viewed as negative aspects of herself. Her reformulated view of self and emotions moved Rose toward freedom: "Freedom in my mental health is closely aligned with the freedom that God offers."[26]

Jason's Step Toward Redemption

Like Rose, Jason had a similar journey of insight into God's call to freedom. Time at RDM led Jason to increased self-acceptance, emotional growth, and spiritual awareness. Jason connected God's presence and love with his sense of purpose. Although we started the counseling process honoring Jason's request for a strictly secular perspective, he brought his spirituality and view of God into later sessions: "It helped me truly understand how much God loved me for who I was despite what I thought of myself and it helped me realize that I was created very uniquely and . . . with intent. Like, to be, with purpose, on purpose."[27] Counseling at RDM brought to life a faith and connection with God that Jason had previously neglected.

25. Rose, interview by author, July 6, 2017.
26. Rose, interview by author, July 6, 2017.
27. Jason, interview by author, July 15, 2017.

Transformations in Red Door Ministry

In one session, Jason recalled dreams and images with spiritual significance that had repeated over the course of his life. Jason connected these images with God's invitation for him to "Be Still" during overwhelming times in his life. Jason explained: "these are really important words to me because ... there was a lot of chaos and a lot of noise and ... there was just a lot of anxiety and I dunno, those words will ring in my mind forever."[28] When all the other external oppressive voices placed heavy burdens and pressures on Jason to succeed and perform, God's voice provided peace and rest. This peace and rest served as a call to trust and let God lead the dance in Jason's life.

Like Rose, Jason's realization of God's love helped him to identify the redemptive elements of his life and his position on the margins. A renewed affirmation of God's love and the call to "Be Still" helped Jason face his fears as well: "It helped me realize how big God was and how little like some things are, like my fears ... the fear of not being successful became very small to me."[29] The authoritative, oppressive voices that increased Jason's anxiety became much smaller in comparison to the gentle whispers of divine love and purpose in his life. By opening himself up to the movement of God, Jason found affirmation in what he had always valued: "The things that I always thought [were] important in life, like being there for people, or trying to make people happy or loving people, or accepting people, those became much bigger and much more acceptable to me."[30] His fears and anxiety that originally came from being placed on the margins by oppressive systems subsided as Jason identified a new call to form positive, meaningful relationships. Jason saw himself and the purpose of his life with new eyes as he joined God in prioritizing connecting with all people, both in the center and on the margins.

Rose and Jason realized the gentleness and love with which God sees and calls them. Seeing themselves as God's unique and precious creation quieted the oppressive voices and the fears that accompanied them. They tuned into their creator's voice as God created a place of safety, acceptance, and love for their own voices to grow in volume. Their theological insights shifted their attention from the anxieties and restrictions of being on the margins to a focus on seeing the redemptive value of their identity and their social locations. These two clients' new ways of seeing themselves propelled

---

28. Jason, interview by author, July 15, 2017
29. Jason, interview by author, July 15, 2017
30. Jason, interview by author, July 15, 2017

them to places of freedom and new life. This new insight helped Rose and Jason move to the next step of challenging the oppressive systems that were in place in their lives.

Step 4: Using Redemptive Elements to Challenge Oppressive Systems

The redemptive ways of seeing themselves and their unique positions in their communities allowed SGKA clients Rose and Jason to raise their voices against the oppressive systems that previously kept them on the margins. Their refusal to remain in quiet submission to oppressive voices slowly brought them out of the margins. How can marginalized groups challenge and impact the center? Can they expand or become the center?

The Fluidity of Margins and Centers

Our analysis of margins and centers has so far been conducted as if these two positions were distinct and separate from each other. Deeper examination, however, shows center and margin to be intricately connected and fluid. In *Theological Reflections on "Gangnam Style,"* Joseph Cheah and Grace J. Kim examine the connection between margins and centers. Taking the popular K-pop song "Gangnam Style"[31] as an example, they argue that something new, created outside the center, can impact and change the center itself. The song's international popularity slowly moved those in the Western center to be exposed to a culture and language without a need for translation. As those in the center turn to this new creation from the margins, embracing the song, they gather around what becomes a new center: "As Asian Americans continue to struggle with marginalization . . . it is important to recognize that the marginalization imposed by the dominant culture can be cracked or penetrated. The popularity of "Gangnam Style" attest to this possibility."[32] In the same way that "Gangnam Style" and other K-pop songs took the world by storm, those living on the margins can offer a new perspective and with "authenticity and imagination"[33] can radically

---

31. It must be noted that much of the song's fame initially came from the West laughing at the musical styles and outlandish visuals and dance of the music video which builds upon over a century's worth of racial stereotype of Asian men.

32. Cheah and Kim, *Theological Reflections on "Gangnam Style,"* 80.

33. Cheah and Kim, *Theological Reflections on "Gangnam Style,"* 76.

change the center. In their continued struggle with marginalization, SGKAs can challenge the oppressive center from where they stand, hoping that the center can be impacted by those in the margins.

The example of "Gangnam Style" and its piercing of the center raises questions as to how the margins and centers inform one another:

> It is sometimes difficult to differentiate between centrality and marginality as they are dependent upon the subject and the object's perspective, and are comparative to the cultural context in which the ranking of identity takes place. It is important, therefore, to understand the relativity of multiple centers and margins.[34]

The delineation of centers and margins is dependent on contexts and perspectives. I want to push this idea further and propose that both centers and margins are fluid spaces that can expand and contract. New centers can emerge from the margins, and centers can become margins. SGKAs can find themselves in the center in one context and can be pushed to the margins in another. Their experience of marginalization, however, must inform any new centers that they create to ensure that there are no oppressive forces at work for those on the margins.

By accepting God's invitation to the divine dance, those on the margins can move from passive discontent to active resistance as they become agents of change. Theologian Sang Hyun Lee encourages Korean Americans to see marginalization as a liminal space that has the potential to become "creative space of resistance and solidarity."[35] Korean Americans can also work toward creating multiple centers that shed prior oppressive colonial forces and radiate unique strengths and perspectives that reflect the freedom and abundance of life God promises.[36] With multiple centers, Korean Americans can flow in and out of centrality and marginality, benefitting and changing from the various perspectives each center represents. This kind of openness and fluidity requires courage and willingness to step outside set, comfortable boundaries to deepen one's understanding of God and neighbor.

---

34. Cheah and Kim, *Theological Reflections on "Gangnam Style,"* 71.

35. Lee, *From a Liminal Place*, 5.

36. " The thief comes only to steal and kill and destroy. I came that they may have life, and have it abundantly." John 10:10.

Opening the Red Door

God and the Margins

SGKAs and other marginalized groups must recognize how God values and works through those on the margins to bring about God's plan for the centers of this world: "Jesus was radical in the frequency with which He associated himself with the marginalized, the oppressed, and the foreigners."[37] He did not choose his disciples from the Romans who were a powerful and influential nation bent on colonizing the world at that time. Rather, Jesus found company among the marginalized Galileans living under imperialistic rule. These oppressed and powerless people joined a divine dance and were empowered to courageously bring a new message of hope, love, freedom, and salvation throughout the Roman empire. What started out on the margins, slowly penetrated the center, creating a new global religion. The Galileans challenged the beliefs and cultures of the center and introduced a radical new force that changed Roman culture and all subsequent Western history. Lee claims:

> God chooses the liminal margins of this world as the strategic place to begin God's decisive work of carrying out God's own end in creation. God chooses to work through liminal/marginalized people in order to love and redeem all fallen humanity. This is because marginalized people . . . possess a more heightened liminality . . . thus a little more openness to God's good news.[38]

RDM clients exhibited heightened sensitivity and awareness of their liminal marginality as they showed resistance to the oppressive systems that kept them and others on the margins.

Challenging Oppressive Voices in Red Door Ministry

Ava Challenges Oppressive Systems

Ava's progress in self-love and self-care for her physical, emotional, and spiritual self came from confronting and challenging the oppressive systemic worldviews she had heard throughout her life. Her first confrontation was with the internalized voices that devalued her emotions, her physical body, and her worth. Her journey at RDM opened her eyes to see God "like a father, [sic] . . . he's [sic] hurting when [I] say or think these things that I

37. Cheah and Kim, *Theological Reflections on "Gangnam Style,"* 89.
38. Lee, *From a Liminal Place*, 35.

think . . . so he [sic] seems more gentler."³⁹ This gentler view of God gave Ava permission to be gentler with herself and appreciate who she is and where she stands in society. She saw herself as a child of God whose words and thoughts deeply matter to God. God's tenderness and kindness led Ava to challenge the strict oppressive voices within her, replacing them with new appreciation for her beauty and value.

No longer captive to the narrow views of what society deemed worthy, Ava found her significance and beauty defined by God. She showed active participation in learning the dance steps away from the margins and toward the center challenging and changing the biased, oppressive standards of worth and beauty. Ava's view and relationship with God empowered her to say, "I am becoming more important,"⁴⁰ redeeming her worth and value.

Ava's struggles with body image and feelings that she was unacceptable also stemmed from oppressive voices from society and media that define a woman's beauty and worth through patriarchal standards. Her feelings and thoughts that she could never physically measure up to society's ideals of beauty slowly faded as she challenged centralized social standards. Ava expressed her newfound appreciation of God's unique designs for all creation:

> It's all different, all different shapes . . . that God created. The trees, the leaves, the lands, the flowers, and everything, and I, I feel like and I don't know if this is what [is] meant by we're all made in his [sic] image, but tall, short, we're all perfect in our own way.⁴¹

Ava's identification as one created by God meant that she started to see herself as beautiful. Her change of perspective also meant that she also began to see others as more beautiful as oppressive standards within herself were challenged.

Sam Challenges Oppressive Systems

Sam's journey in RDM also led him to challenge oppressive systems that previously constricted and limited him from freely expressing himself. Like the other clients, Sam found affirmation of his value and complexity. He embraced these redemptive elements as pathways to help him understand God's love and will for him:

39. Ava, interview by author, July 5, 2017.
40. Ava, interview by author, July 5, 2017.
41. Ava, interview by author, July 5, 2017.

> [God] created me into being so unique, so different and you know I've got my own quirks, my own different things that I enjoy doing and different things I hate or [am] at peace [with] and it's so complex! Even how I think is different from other people or the kinds of thoughts are so different, it's so complex it's so unique that it makes me, it helps me understand that God loves me in a personal way.[42]

The differences and "quirks" that he previously tried to hide or limit due to feelings of marginalization have now become badges of pride and confidence that proved God's personal love toward Sam. This redemptive view of himself led Sam to become "like a warrior. Before, I would kind of run away from things but I've realized lately that I, uh, I dunno, I seem to have more, like grit . . . I'm persevering more."[43] He engaged in battle as a warrior against the oppressive voices as he asserted his own thoughts and feelings: "I don't have to pretend, I don't have to act, I can just be myself, umm, I dunno, it feels more natural."[44] Sam's recognition of his own complexity could lead to his recognition and appreciation of the complexity of all others. By partnering with God in the divine dance, Sam has left the margins to live in the center of his life where his uniqueness and complexities are celebrated.

In the introduction of this book, I defined *center* as the *space* where people are empowered to live as complex human beings whose experiences and contributions are seen and valued by society. Seeing the *other* as complex human beings prevents marginalized treatment. By embracing all people as valuable, unique, and dignified, we can live as agents with power. The SGKA clients showed this agency in the next step they partnered with God.

Step 5: Owning Power and Agency

Power

Considerations of the relationships between margins and center are not complete without discussing the role of power. As we have seen in step 2, an initial differentiation that Hurley gives for center and margin is "a powerful [center] and a less powerful margin."[45] Although his argument continues

---

42. Sam, interview by author, June 29, 2017.
43. Sam, interview by author, June 29, 2017.
44. Sam, interview by author, June 29, 2017.
45. Hurley. "Who's on Whose Margins," 178.

Transformations in Red Door Ministry

by complicating this simplified analysis, the power differentials between the two cannot be ignored. Hurley goes on to declare that "[t]he margins are not always powerless."[46] Rather, marginalized people form their own cultures that are often not determined by the center. This refusal to let the center dictate the margins parallels bell hooks' explanation of power:

> One of the most significant forms of power held by the weak is "the refusal to accept the definition of oneself that is put forward by the powerful.". . . [They] need to know that they can reject the powerful's definition of their reality—that they can do so even if they are poor, exploited or trapped in oppressive circumstances. They need to know that the exercise of this basic personal power is an act of resistance and strength.[47]

This exercise of personal power is the starting point for change. By rejecting the one-dimensional view or the dehumanizing gaze oppressive systems place on marginalized groups, those on the margins no longer give up power over their own sense of self.

Those on the margins must refuse to accept oppressive voices. There is liberation and a sense of agency when marginalized people recreate a new reality where they live as complex, powerful people who resist oppression. There is no doubt that oppressive voices exist, demanding submission and silence from the margins. Internalizing these voices perpetuates and heightens the damage for the marginalized by taking away their personal power. Resisting these harmful voices and nurturing their own voices can elicit a strong sense of power and agency for those on the margins. They must develop a different definition of themselves, using their own voices, that comes from self-discovery and from partnering with God. There is much power and strength that comes from knowing who they are and what they can offer the world.

RDM clients have found new power in their places of marginality as they reclaim their voices and agency. Cheah and Kim state: "the margin . . . becomes a powerful site of resistance to the center. This site of creativity is a place where we recognize that marginalized voices can be heard, acknowledged, and celebrated."[48] As RDM clients' counseling processes continue to unfold, some have chosen to resist their oppressive centers by physically

---

46. Hurley. "Who's on Whose Margins," 179.
47. hooks, *Feminist Theory*, 92.
48. Cheah and Kim, *Theological Reflections on "Gangnam Style,"* 73.

taking themselves out of these places. They partner with God to build their own centers where their power and voice are celebrated.

Jason's Power and Agency

As seen in chapter 3, Jason took the freedom and sense of agency he discovered in RDM to make a significant move in his life. Rather than letting outside forces define who he should be and what he should do, Jason moved to a new state, pursued a new career, and formed new friends that reflected who he defined himself to be. This new chapter of Jason's life is marked with freedom and happiness. He joined God's dance in this relocation that produced the new life sprouting forth in his emotional and spiritual life. He described this move: "It's something I never would have done if I had never gone to Red Door Ministry . . . you don't understand how happy I am living here . . . it symbolizes home . . . where I belong . . . it's what I wanted my whole life, but like I just never got here. I never knew."[49] By listening and actively putting into practice his renewed faith and understanding of God, Jason was empowered to move out of oppression into a new place of freedom. He continued: "I believed. I was super scared, but I believed, I had faith that . . . I was going home, which is weird, but that's how I felt."[50] Jason's reclaiming of power and bold action in following God's call resulted in a feeling of finding and going home. For Jason, home was a place he felt true belonging with the power and freedom to be himself. Home became a place where he felt centered and no longer on the margins. It was a place where Jason chose new relationships and practiced new ways of staying in relationships.

Jeong

Owning power and agency means the RDM clients have chosen new ways of relating to and staying in relationships with oppressive systems as well as with others on the margins. Although not explicitly named as such within the walls of RDM, clients used the practice of *jeong* in this step of their transformation. Chapter 3 looked at *jeong* as a concept with which clients have confronted their shame. In outlining the steps of the holy dance in RDM, *jeong*'s significance is seen again. This relationality of "compassion,

---

49. Jason, interview by author, July 15, 2017.
50. Jason, interview by author, July 15, 2017.

love, vulnerability, and acceptance of heterogeneity"[51] is the power that takes clients from claiming their redemptive identities to confronting and transforming the evils of oppression as agents of change and love.

Realizing that those on the margins and centers are connected in the mutual experiences of sorrow, suffering, and longing, as well as in joy, love, and compassion make *jeong* possible. Seeing the humanity of each person leads the clients and other marginalized groups to repent for their own shortcomings as well as to forgive others for theirs. As clients and others move toward new centers, *jeong* reminds them of the common humanity we all share as we create new "traditions of cherishing each other . . . [that] can thaw the icy conditions"[52] between those in the center and those in the margins.

Sam's Jeong

By understanding and experiencing more of God's love and *jeong* toward him, Sam proclaimed his willingness to extend *jeong* to those around them. As his view of God and Jesus became more personal, Sam began to see relationality and *jeong* as significant markers of love. Sam saw Jesus as one who chose to be amongst the messiness of intimate relationships with each person. Sam described this shift in perspective:

> It's the idea of choosing love. I think before I always thought Jesus never was impatient or you know . . . like he never got impatient or angry, like, the emotions that I tend to equate with someone who's human and not perfect. But I think, if that was the case . . . him being patient and him not showing anger and all those different things . . . the idea of love doesn't make sense because, if I'm not given a moment where I can choose impatience, then am I really choosing to love? Am I loving?[53]

Sam's use of the term "love" reflected more of the tensions that exist in the concept of *jeong*. The complex emotion of *jeong* allows for compassion, vulnerability, love, anger, recognition of injustice, and power to coexist. Jesus' choice of staying in relationship with and loving people despite pain and suffering, ultimately seen on the cross, served as the point where violence,

---

51. Joh, *Heart of the Cross*, xxi.
52. Park, *Racial Conflict and Healing*, 116.
53. Sam, interview by author, June 29, 2017.

oppression, love, and power converge. The cross therefore became an event "signifying a risk that one encounters as one lives in the fullness of *jeong*."[54]

Previously, Sam saw Jesus as someone removed from any human emotions and as one who conceptually represented love. With a more personalized view, Sam saw both the humanity and divinity of Christ, as well as the interconnectedness God chose to be in with human beings. By realizing and understanding more of the deep *jeong* Christ showed, Sam decided to extend it to others by "choosing to love, choosing to be patient, choosing to serve,"[55] even if others hurt him or failed him. This choosing to be in relationship showed Sam's willingness to stay in conflict and complex situations, the very definition of *jeong*.

Sam's choice of *jeong* reflected the power and agency he started to own in RDM. Others around Sam have noticed this change in him:

> [P]eople have made comments like "You're more confident or you're more positive." I can kind of tell too . . . I guess it's the result of being in here and understanding my own self-worth, and, umm, understanding like how God views me, but I've been very confident in myself to the point where like I wonder if I'm like being like arrogant . . . I know that it comes from the one who gifted it to me . . . and I'm going to use it to serve people more, to show love to others.[56]

Connecting with others through *jeong* shows powerful agency that requires a constant relationship with God for continued guidance and inspiration. Doing so can help SGKA clients like Sam stay in relationship with others on the margins for unity and strength and those at the center for dialogue and transformation. From these relationships co-creating new, liberating centers of hope, empowerment, justice, and self-discovery become possible. These new centers can become places where marginalized people feel fully welcome, find belonging, and claim as their home.

---

54. Joh, *Heart of the Cross*, 84.
55. Sam, interview by author, June 29, 2017.
56. Sam, interview by author, June 29, 2017.

Step 6: Co-Creating New Centers

Chi

The steps outlined in this chapter started with the Holy Spirit's invitation to join in the divine dance that would create room for openness and possibilities. This sixth step of co-creating new centers circles back to the Holy Spirit in a slightly different way. The importance of recognizing the influence of both Eastern and Western traditions and worldviews in SGKA clients challenges us to consider a richer, hybrid view of God's spirit. Bringing together both traditional Eastern and Western views on new life and transformation can form a deeper, more meaningful theology for SGKAs that speaks to their in-between and marginalized existence.

Grace Ji-Sun Kim does this in her introduction of the Eastern concept of *chi* and its relationship to the Holy Spirit. She aims to expand our understanding of God's work for those living in hybrid spaces by placing *chi* and Holy Spirit together. Kim defines *chi*:

> Chi does not have a specific form, instead, it is revealed in the change, transformation, and movement of things. Chi is only the movement and never the form. Furthermore, Chi is identified with the creation of life and with all the things in the process of change. Chi has infinite possibilities and in the boundless source of change.[57]

Chi is a fundamental concept in Eastern medicine and martial arts. Often described as the flow of energy, *chi* refers to both the physical and beyond: "Chi has healing powers that can bring new life and energy to damaged bodies and persons. It has been understood and used as a juncture for healing in the Eastern tradition for many years."[58] Kim's emphasis of *chi* as movement, change, healing, and new life compliments the metaphoric dance we are using to understand God and the clients' relationship with the divine in their transformation.

The Eastern understandings of *chi* as "the force of life that has always been existent, an important force within our universe giving and sustaining all life"[59] are also remarkably similar to the theological view of the Holy Spirit. The increase in energy and liveliness that the clients depicted in this

---

57. Kim, *Holy Spirit, Chi*, 17.
58. Kim, *Holy Spirit, Chi*, 17
59. Kim, *Holy Spirit, Chi*, 12.

step reflects their renewed and strengthened *chi* as they participate in the divine movement. This hybrid understanding of the Holy Spirit unites not only the Eastern with the Western perspectives of the clients, but also connects the spiritual, psychological, emotional, and physical aspects within them. This holistic approach to healing and transformation reflects the experiences of the four clients.

Chi and New Centers

The transformation and movement of *chi* is evident throughout all the steps of the divine dance but is especially made manifest in this last step of co-creation. *Chi* took the clients from owning their power and agency to using them in forming new centers where they could move, breathe, and live in boundless possibilities. The clients' arrival at this step of transformation brought them to a place of creative possibilities of change. To understand how the clients' renewed *chi* led them to changes and to possibilities of co-creation with God, I asked them to give a piece of advice or wisdom that they have gained from their journey. Each client gave a proverb that continues to keep them open to the flow of *chi* and to wherever the next steps partnering with God might take them.

Co-Creating New Centers in Red Door Ministry

Ava's Center of Hope

Ava was quick to give her advice: "Don't give up hope . . . there will be better days, guaranteed."[60] Ava was unique among the clients because she had several years of previous counseling experience from two counselors that she claimed did not help her. In fact, she recalled feeling frustrated and confused when there was no change being made and even worse when her previous counselor terminated her after two years of a static therapeutic relationship. In desperation, Ava gave counseling a third chance. This tenacity of spirit and determination for change brought Ava to RDM where she accepted God's invitation to move her through the steps of transformation. Going through the six steps has brought her to the current place of "better days." Ava added: "You can give up after you try all the options (pause) five times

---

60. Ava, interview by author, July 5, 2017.

(laughter)."[61] No matter how painful, dark, and winding the path has been, Ava never gave up hope. She never stopped looking for better possibilities. By saying "yes" to God's invitation to embark on another leg of counseling in her journey, her hope was fulfilled. As Ava continues to confront oppressive systems and perspectives, she can turn to her own advice of never giving up hope. Her movement from desperation to "better days" reflects *chi*'s current in her life which now overflows to others as she invites them to accept God's invitation and join her in this hopeful place away from the margins.

Ava also addressed how she had reclaimed her cultural heritage as a source of power to create change. She encouraged other SGKAs to do the same:

> For me, as a *Korean* American . . . [I am] not ashamed. Like, be very . . . grounded in who you are as a person . . . And then use the fact that you're a second generation to, I dunno, bring about change and yeah maybe for me it's the workplace . . . so you know, just believing [that] if you do something that it will [have] a ripple effect or something. Just believe whatever you do will create change.[62]

Ava took her identity as a SGKA that used to be the basis of harsh bullying by others and reclaimed it as her strength and source of power. She no longer felt ashamed of her heritage but used the benefits of being between multiple cultures to see more and create change. By accepting herself first and learning to value her own voice, Ava became an advocate for her patients and friends who may also struggle to have their voices heard.

Rose's Center of Empowerment and Justice

Rose's advice for SGKAs echoed Ava's reclaiming of her heritage and voice:

> I think that it's important to, umm, to be who you are . . . even if there is a collide of cultures and, umm, I think that for almost all [SGKAs] that I know, our voice has been diminished and our voice has been put aside in many ways because our passions aren't heard. And I think that if you want to be who you are you have to like not be afraid of your own voice, go and be who you are, and not allow the fear of failure determine how you live your life.[63]

---

61. Ava, interview by author, July 5, 2017.
62. Ava, interview by author, July 5, 2017.
63. Rose, interview by author, July 6 2017.

This wisdom reflected her journey of reclaiming her voice and living a life more empowered to be who she was created to be. Rose used her painful experience of being marginalized to make sure that the new center she co-creates with God has no room for oppressive forces. She wanted to ensure inclusivity and diversity, where no one feels marginalized. The new life and energy that *chi* brought to Rose gave her the courage to address the first-generation Korean Americans who have marginalized her:

> Don't use your power to like boss us around, be nice to us. I think there was so much emphasis on what we can offer and what we can do . . . instead of focusing on who we are and what was special about us and a part of that is just like being available, being humble and that's a lot of ask for like first generation Korean Americans . . . There's a lot of pride in how they grew up and things that they've suffered from that they feel like they have this power over us because of what they've experienced and like, how much they've gone through to be where they are, but that doesn't give them permission to, umm, like boss us around or make us feel less adequate because of an experience they've had.[64]

As the only client to address both the SGKAs and the first-generation Korean Americans in her interview, Rose made concrete one of the sources of marginalization that the other participants merely implied.

First-generation Korean Americans have oppressed and hurt SGKAs in deep ways. Rose's words were also a cry for justice and a demand for SGKAs to be seen as valuable, complex human beings, rather than as a group of people seen as existing to serve the first generation. Rose understood that the first generation's marginalization of SGKAs is connected to the first-generation Korean Americans' own feelings of marginalization from American society. The suffering and pain of the first generation cannot serve as the reason for them to pass the same pain of marginalization on to their children, the second generation. When marginalized populations create new centers where power and agency are reclaimed, they have to be extremely cautious that they are not repeating similar patterns of oppression and marginalization in these new places. This possibility requires a constant self-critique and evaluation that comes from continued self-discovery.

---

64. Rose, interview by author, July 6 2017

Transformations in Red Door Ministry

Sam's Center of Self-Discovery

Sam's wisdom called for deeper self-discovery and evaluation of the lives of SGKAs to find purpose and meaning. Sam said,

> Don't take your circumstances, your experiences too lightly, 'cuz all those things do play a role and effect how you end up . . . Self-discovery, learning about yourself, it's going to be important to everyone. I almost want to say that it's even more important for [SGKAs] to do that because of, you know, the kind of confusion they may go through exposed to multiple cultures.[65]

Sam reiterated not only the value of the SGKA experience but also the impact of self-discovery in their relationships and "how you end up." Sam's renewed energy for life and relationships that came from the flow of *chi* helped him to realize the important role and effects of self-discovery. His advice to SGKAs called for a shift in perspective, to turn confusion into understanding and marginalization into centrality.

Jason's Center of Freedom

Jason took the idea of self-discovery a bit further when he encouraged others to move beyond societal expectations and pursue what brings them new life:

> Do as you want to do, you know? Do what makes you happy, like don't worry about what other people are doing. Go! . . . 'cuz a lot of people are doing things they don't want to do, especially Korean Americans. They do what's expected of them, or studying in a field that is kind of imposed, I dunno. Everyone needs to take the time to step out of [it] . . . Put your whole life on hold and you need to really think [about these] things.[66]

Jason's advice came from his own discovery of freedom when he rejected the heavy pressures and expectations that previously chained him down with guilt and shame for falling short. His understanding of God was a liberating force that invited him to rest and "Be Still." In this stillness, Jason found reenergized *chi* that empowered him to carve out his own path.

---

65. Sam, interview by author, June 29 2017.
66. Jason, interview by author, July 15, 2017.

By partnering with God to build these new centers from the margins, these clients have become the main actors in their lives. Through hope, empowerment, justice, self-discovery, and freedom, they continue to affirm their value, expanding new centers by inviting others to join in the divine dance.

The Flow of Divine Movement

When marginalized groups are not allowed to fully participate in or contribute to the life of various centers, their bodies, minds, emotions, and spirits suffer. Power is often taken away as they are pushed to the margins of their communities and the larger American society. They can feel stuck, hopeless, and angry. God enters these marginal places and extends God's hand as an invitation to join in the divine dance. Scripture and history show many examples of God standing with the marginalized and oppressed and empowering them to move toward hope, empowerment, justice, self-discovery, and freedom. SGKAs are uniquely positioned in contemporary times as they stand in similar places of marginalization.

Moving from the margins to co-creating new centers has been outlined in this chapter in six steps: God is inviting marginalized people to be

1. Open to creative possibilities by joining in the divine dance;
2. Accepting God's invitation helps them identify and address the oppressive systems in their lives;
3. God then opens their eyes to identify redemptive elements of their identity and social position, and they begin to see their value and worth through God's perspective;
4. These redemptive elements are then used to challenge the oppressive systems as;
5. They own power and reclaim agency; and
6. Empowered by partnering with God, they co-create new centers.

As these steps are taken, marginalized people bring new perspectives and new life not only in their own lives and their own community but also to the larger society. They can live prophetic lives as they take responsibility, ownership, and agency to bring about the much-needed changes God reveals to them. Their co-creation of new centers can bring new understandings and fresh waves of God's love and justice beyond any one community.

Chapter 5 will imagine how the divine activities seen in RDM can be extended beyond its walls.

5

Going Beyond the Red Door Ministry

THE PREVIOUS CHAPTERS HAVE explored how RDM provides pastoral care and counseling for SGKAs who struggle to find home in both the Korean American community and American society. Four clients lend their voices to describe their personal transformations from living in shame on the margins to flourishing in newly created centers. This concluding chapter begins with my hopes for these clients as they move beyond RDM. How can they take the changes they found at RDM beyond its walls? How can they move beyond shame and co-create new centers outside the counseling space? Next, I will consider how the theories and frameworks used in RDM can be extended for the care of the larger Korean American community and other marginalized populations. How can the spaces of RDM be extended to encompass an entire community? How can these elements and environments be passed down to the third and fourth generations? Finally, I explore the role of counselors, caregivers, and community leaders beyond RDM. How does my experience of RDM as a counselor and pastoral theologian aid in unlocking more doors for the creation of empowering spaces?

The Clients: Beyond the Red Door Ministry

Taking the Red Door Ministry Beyond Its Walls

All four clients from this study entered RDM cautiously and discretely. They were "wary about telling anybody that [they were] in counseling."[1] By the time of the interviews, however, they had all become strong proponents of counseling and of RDM. Since then, the clients have shared with others testimonies of their transformations with boldness and conviction. Courageously using their own stories, these RDM clients have paved the way for other SGKAs and persons of different cultural backgrounds to embark on their own paths toward wholeness at RDM.

RDM clients are becoming agents of change that influence their families, friends, and communities. As their testimonials spread, their shame continues to diminish and their renewed confidence gains recognition and ripples of change spread throughout their spheres of influence. Through a renewed fervor of empowerment and creativity, I hear their hopes and visions of systemic change. In *Moving Beyond Individualism in Pastoral Care and Counseling,* Barbara McClure explains the connection between personal transformation and systemic change:

> personal transformation will not change the system, however, it is an indispensable requirement to systemic change, and vice versa. Indeed, individual transformation can never be fully realized without the transformation of the evil dimensions of the systems within which we come into being, live our lives, and develop our values and identities.[2]

Although individual RDM client transformations cannot immediately overturn systemic injustices, the clients' heightened awareness of empowerment and agency can impact relationships and communities in close proximity to them. All the clients from this study have taken their reclaimed voices and power to dream and create unique spaces of new centers.

---

1. Rose, interview by author, July 6, 2017.
2. McClure, *Moving Beyond Individualism*, 219.

Opening the Red Door

Clients Creating Space

Ava's Dream: Creating Potential Space for Justice

In her job as a nurse, Ava has become a better advocate for self-care, for justice for her family, and for equity for her patients. Ava is actively working hard to create new patterns of self-care and rest. She has stepped out of her role as the "good child" and has expressed her true feelings and thoughts to her sisters and mother as a reflection of her true self. In times of stress, however, her old patterns of devaluing her needs still surface, but she is aware of this tendency and works hard to prevent it.

Lately, Ava's sessions have centered around the injustices she sees in the way patients are treated at the hospital where she works. She is troubled when she sees that patients are cared for with indifference or even viewed as a nuisance by some of her co-workers. As an advocate for these patients, Ava has approached her supervisors and peers. She has also turned to social media as an outlet to explore this issue. I am noticing Ava's increasing desire to use her gentle, yet strong voice, the voice that she has uncovered at RDM, to speak for patients and for their quality of care.

In a recent session, Ava shared her dream of creating a workshop for nurses that could help prevent compassion fatigue[3] and burn out. As I walked her through her dream, Ava played with the idea of creating a potential space where nurses could hear from past patients and their families in an open and trusting environment. She imagined a safe space where a "dream team" of nurses could meaningfully connect with patients as complex, full human beings in an environment where both could engage in creative activity to consider improved ways of care. Ava dreamed of bringing nurses and patients together as "whole" people to challenge the transactional relationships that pattern many of the patient-provider interactions at the hospital where she works. Ava's dream of taking the transformations she made at RDM beyond its walls to create new spaces of care for others speaks of RDM's utility for cultivating dreams for individual and systemic change. My hope is to see the success of Ava's continued advocacy and her efforts to make her dreams become a reality.

---

3. Defined as "apathy or indifference towards the suffering of others or to charitable causes acting on their behalf, typically attributed to numbingly frequent appeals for assistance, esp. donations; (hence) a diminishing public response to frequent charitable appeals." From *Oxford English Dictionary Online*, s.v. "Compassion Fatigue, N.," accessed July 26, 2018.

Going Beyond the Red Door Ministry

Rose's Ministry: Creating Space for Jeong

Rose has created a new space beyond the walls of RDM where people gather to worship and care for one another. Since her time at RDM, Rose has started a house church with several people, of which she is the lead. Her renewed confidence to start this ministry was invigorated through conversations at RDM about recovering and affirming her voice as a minister. As discussed in previous chapters, because of the patriarchy in many Korean American Christian contexts, Rose still struggles to have her ministerial voice heard and be taken seriously. In facing these systemic and patriarchal injustices, Rose also confronts her own bitterness and aggression toward others.

Currently, Rose is practicing *jeong* as she considers those who may have different experiences from her. As Rose confronts her own pain of being unheard, she wrestles with the idea of how she might remain in healthy relationship with those who hold such patriarchal views. *Jeong* keeps her connected as she recognizes that abandoning these relationships is not an option. By choosing *jeong*, Rose creates new ways of connecting and loving others while she attends to her pain. Rose also continues to create unique spaces within herself where self-compassion allows her to address her bitterness and aggression with vulnerability and courage. Wonhee Anne Joh connects *jeong* with vulnerability: "Foremost, *jeong* challenges and demands vulnerability from ourselves. By ultimately asking for vulnerability, we are challenged to go beyond ourselves."[4] My hope is to see Rose build upon the new spaces she has made where *jeong* and vulnerability form new centers of empowerment.

Jason's Next Chapter: Creating Space for Hahn

Jason took the freedom and faith he uncovered in RDM and used it as the foundation for a new chapter in life. Following his move to a new state, Jason applied and interviewed for a full-time position in an area of his interests. Facing one of his greatest sources of fear and anxiety with hope and courage, he secured the position and now enjoys working in this new environment. Jason's openness to face his fears and pursue his dream, which surfaced at RDM, reflects *hahn*, which "epitomizes the openness of life."[5]

---

4. Joh, *Heart of the Cross*, 122.
5. Park, *Racial Conflict and Healing*, 115.

Jason also opened his heart so he could reconcile with his brother and his father toward whom he previously held deep grudges and anger. The hate he carried in his heart melted away as his own self-hatred diminished through his counseling process. Jason's openness can also be seen in his changed attitude and acceptance of people he previously judged negatively: "A really big thing here is, the closest friend I made here is a gay guy. I never in my life thought I would have a gay friend and I'm actually moving into his house in like two weeks."[6] His conservative upbringing was challenged and overturned by his own voice and love of people.

Jason's openness to others adds wisdom and strength to his voice as he co-creates a more loving, and open world around him. This "openness . . . is not a condition but a direction toward which [he is] moving. [His] future is not determined but open and unfolding."[7] With a future open to new possibilities, Jason has committed to listening to his voice and soliciting the wisdom of others. My hope for Jason is that his open embrace of different people and situations will create a future full of majestic *hahn* and deep, meaningful relationships.

Sam's Renewed Energy: Creating Space for Authenticity

Sam has embraced a leadership role within his church and has claimed that he does not feel burned out in serving as he did prior to coming to RDM. Relationships continue to remain a priority for Sam, which he nurtures through friendships and ministry. Sam now connects more genuinely with others because he is no longer constricting himself to fit into an imagined ideal. He has also quit his job as a mechanical engineer to pursue a profession in which he finds more joy and purpose. Sam's faith, openness, and optimism for his future have been met with a new job in his chosen field. Both Sam's relationships and his shift in occupation reflect his value of authenticity.

Sam has renewed vigor to immerse himself in community and to allow himself to be truly known by others. He is avoiding the easier route of seeing others through flattened stereotypes. Sam is now fully engaging in the hard work of loving others as complex human beings. By doing so, he gleans from the wisdom and experiences of his relationships and widens his worldview. My hope is that Sam will continue to engage in self-critique,

---

6. Jason, interview by author, November 12, 2017.
7. Park, *Racial Conflict and Healing*, 105.

to challenge conformity, and to reevaluate imagined expectations and ideals as he pursues his calling.

Ava, Rose, Jason, and Sam demonstrate the ripple effects of how personal transformation in a counseling space can catalyze change and galvanize the creation of liberating spaces. How can spaces like RDM be brought outside the limits of a counseling room? How can we empower more individuals to bring changes in our communities and in the systems of which we are a part? What kind of space can address the pain and suffering of marginalized individuals and groups in current times as well as for the generations to come?

The Community: Beyond the Red Door Ministry

SGKAs and other marginalized groups need caregivers who will stand with them in empowering spaces and help them challenge oppression. This solidarity starts with an awareness of the unbalance of power that has readily been accepted as the norm in society. A reevaluation must also take place that not only deconstructs unjust systems but also examines one's complicity and participation with injustice. To this end, caregivers must be vigilant about how oppression makes its way into their practice of care. They must continually engage in deep introspection and self-evaluation to uproot vestiges of racism and sexism within themselves as well as in the therapeutic space.

At RDM, space is made for the creation of new, liberating centers of justice, *jeong, hahn,* and authenticity. SGKAs and other marginalized populations in need of healing from marginalization are free to join God in co-creating new centers where their lives and the lives of the generations that will follow can flourish. In this work of co-creation, I now turn to scripture and postcolonial theory to imagine the elements that make up such liberating spaces.

A Scriptural Model for Flourishing Space

The Parable of the Sower: Space for Growth and Healing

In Matthew 13:3–9, Christ tells the parable of the sower. Although Christ explains the parable as a symbolic representation of our heart and its openness to receive God's truth, we can find value in broadening the parable to represent the environment needed for the growth of healthy SGKAs and other marginalized populations. The parable examines four different spaces and environments where the sower went out to sow.

The first group of seeds "fell on the path and the birds came and ate them up."[8] This illustrates the kind of environment in which SGKAs and other marginalized voices are ignored or silenced. They are not given a chance to be "planted," resulting in many SGKAs' leaving or being "picked off" by predatory systems that espouse a hardened, inflexible, and hostile environment. Robbed of any chance to put down roots, SGKAs in this kind of space live with deep wounds in their hearts.

The seeds that fell on rocky ground "sprang up quickly . . . But then the sun rose, they were scorched; and since they had no root, they withered away."[9] Spaces like these initially seem to welcome SGKAs and other marginalized populations, but without continued self-critique and reevaluation of self and the environment, the rocks of bitterness and biases prevent growth. SGKAs and other marginalized groups cannot survive for long. When conflict and hardships come, they are scorched by the sun of marginalization and wither because they have no roots. With their hearts brittle and closed off, SGKAs do not have the inner space or the willingness to work through differences and difficulties, leaving many SGKAs depressed, anxious, and living in unhealthy relationships.

Some seeds also fell "among thorns, and the thorns grew up and choked them."[10] These spaces have the "thorns" of oppressive and marginalizing forces that block SGKAs from flourishing and choke their growth. The evils of racism, sexism, and exclusionism based on differences prevent SGKAs from growing strong because they come up against multiple ceilings that prevent them from reaching their full potential. Although they are given space to be present, SGKAs are limited to non-leadership roles and are kept "in their place."

The last group of seeds "fell on good soil and brought forth grain, some a hundredfold, some sixty, some thirty."[11] This last example depicts the kind of space needed for SGKAs to flourish and to create a nurturing space that can continue into the third and fourth generations of Korean Americans.

Caregivers, leaders, and institutions must encourage and join SGKAs and other marginalized populations as "farmers" who erect scarecrows, pull

8. Matthew 13:4.
9. Matthew 13:5–6.
10. Matthew 13:7.
11. Matthew 13:8.

the thorns, till the ground, and break hard rocks to nurture good, fertile soil. Through continual education, self-critique, and immersion into new cultures and different places, the predators are silenced, rocky hearts are softened, thorny biases are broken, and new growth can begin. In this kind of space for optimal growth and health, SGKAs can "indeed bear . . . fruit and yields in one case a hundredfold, in another sixty, and in another thirty."[12] As a farmer annually prepares the soil, caregivers, leaders, and institutions must also continuously work to create spaces of healing and growth.

The postcolonial concept of third space further examines the elements that are needed for the healing and growth of SGKAs and other marginalized groups.

The Postcolonial Model for Flourishing Space

Third Space

The third space where neither one nor the other dictates but where something else, something new, is created presents the necessary boundary for the formation of empowering new spaces.[13] The multiple voices of caregivers and the care receivers, and the hybrid perspectives of different generations and cultures, come together in the creation of this dynamic space of hope, empowerment, and wisdom. This interactional place where differences are valued and used to create a third space reflects the internal integration and creativity many SGKAs need to embrace the duality of cultures that causes tension and conflict in their lives. Standing in the tension that is created by the binaries within them is the beginning of a third thing, the first steps of integration that lead to the formation of the new. There must, however, be resistance in thinking strictly in binary terms because it can lead to polarization, confusion, and pain.

Third Space and Fusion

The human/sacred, Eastern/Western, marginal/central existence of SGKAs must be brought together in an all embracing third space. This space can form an unshakeable foundation on top of which SGKAs can build an empowering hybrid sense of self that can positively impact the world around

12. Matthew 13:23.
13. See chapter 2 for deeper exploration of Bhabha's concept of third space.

them. Theologian Sang Hyun Lee describes third space as the location where "the colonized person's intentional construction of a hybrid identity and culture can be an activity of resistance to the dominant culture and also an act of forming a new identity and culture."[14] A new identity and a new culture can be constructed by fusing together different elements. Within a third space, the SGKAs can define themselves and resist the shackling identification that is placed upon them. Helena Lee, a SGKA woman, claims:

> Rather than accepting the standard that we all must strive to be like the others, we, as second-generation Korean Americans, can break through the conventional narratives defined by dichotomies of American/Korean, men/women, and twinkie [yellow on the outside, white on the inside]/FOB [Fresh Off the Boat] to create new spaces where all of us can belong as Americans, despite our differences.[15]

This third space goes beyond dichotomies that can emerge by fusing the various elements that previously remained separate. Breaking the conventional narrative requires the skills of fusion where creativity and hybridity form a new counterhegemonic narrative. The creativity and hybridity of fusion cannot emerge without an environment of safety, reliability, acceptance, and trust.

Third Space and Potential Space

Third space must also become a place of play, a potential space where creativity and imagination lead to exploration and an emergence of the new.[16] A reliable space must be made for others to find refuge as they dive into the play of healing, self-discovery, and transformation. I hope the example of RDM as third space and potential space is taken beyond its current scope for the creation of many more such spaces. These spaces will be characterized by the gathering of people from different cultures, backgrounds, and worldviews, spaces where all can become adept and comfortable with standing between multiple spaces, navigating tensions, and embracing complexity. Whether these spaces can be created in schools, in churches, or in other institutions, I can imagine SGKAs and other marginalized groups

---

14. Lee, *From a Liminal Place*, 111.

15. Lee, "*Miyeok guk*," 144.

16. See chapters 2 and 3 for in depth exploration of Winnicott's concept of play, potential space, and creativity.

flourishing in nurturing spaces where their creativity and unique positions and knowledge will bring new life to all around them.

Implications for the Korean American Church

Given the exploration of the kind of space SGKAs and other marginalized populations need for optimal growth and healing, what insights can be given to the institution that is most closely linked with RDM and the place SGKAs turn to most often for care? As discussed in chapter 1, the Korean American immigrant church can act as both comforter and oppressor for SKGAs. What changes and issues must be considered for the Korean American immigrant church to become good soil which yields a bountiful harvest?

SGKAs need a space that will value and use their hybridity to form new ways of worship, ministry, and care. Sharon Kim observes the formation of such churches in her study *A Faith of Our Own*:

> The hybrid third space is born as a response to the lived tensions associated with the sense of discomfort and "not quite fitting in" in either the immigrant or mainstream American religious institutions . . . the hybrid third space is not simply a retreat or refuge from marginalization . . . it is also a place of experimentation, self-definition, and empowerment. Within the third space, second-generation Korean Americans are articulating a hybrid second-generation spirituality and identity. In addition, it is within this hybrid third space that younger Korean Americans are mobilizing to confidently engage and assert their voices in the larger mainstream society.[17]

The churches Sharon Kim studied are in Los Angeles where the number of second and third-generation Korean Americans with deeper American roots is larger compared to the number of Korean Americans living near RDM.

Can such third spaces of worship and care for SGKAs be formed within the Korean America immigrant church? The church where RDM was birthed is an immigrant church with a budding second-generation congregation. Is the future for this second (and third) generation Korean American congregation destined to follow the examples of the churches that Sharon Kim describes above? Are separate congregations the only way such hybrid third spaces form? With the decrease in the number of Korean

17. Kim, *Faith of Our Own*, 14.

immigrants coming each year to the United States and the aging population of first-generation Korean Americans, what does the future of Korean American immigrant churches look like? What will third and fourth-generation Korean Americans need in their churches? In their communities?

The Caregiver: Beyond the Red Door Ministry

Since RDM opened its doors five and a half years ago, I have found myself standing on unstable ground as I have crafted a space for both the clients and myself to heal, grow, and find wholeness. As a female minister and counselor, I have been challenged to break boundaries and to explore fusion and to create a space that was open, trusting, and authentic. In many ways, I have embodied the divided, double-life of homelessness many SGKAs experience. Wedged between the first and second Korean American generations, the academy and the church, the field of psychology and the field of theology, and the Western and Eastern philosophies of understanding human nature and the self, I have found solace in creating RDM. Though I operate in liminality, I can confidently proclaim that my vocation is to create new spaces that encompass neither one or the other but something new from both. RDM has been one such space that supports the healing and empowerment of SGKAs, but I wonder what other spaces caregivers like myself in such liminal spaces might be called on to imagine and create.

The Inner Life of the Dreamer: A Life's Work of Inner Work

It is impossible to create liberating third spaces if caregivers are not committed to self-exploration and liberation. As community leaders and caregivers dream of liberatory worlds, it is imperative that we must also critique our own complicity with injustice and to deconstruct our own acts of oppression. My relationships with RDM clients have challenged my preconceived notions of SGKAs as they teach me and invite me to journey alongside them. These relationships have shaped me to be more open and embracing of new experiences as they stretch my horizons of compassion, patience, and hospitality. RDM clients have also extended my "ability and willingness to attend carefully to . . . day-to-day lived experience, paying close attention to the vicissitudes of everyday life"[18] for my own life. I have experienced

18. McClure, *Moving Beyond Individualism*, 79.

amazing moments of synchronicity when doing so, moments that integrate common themes and events from different areas of my life. I have channeled these significant emerging themes into my efforts to co-create new centers of hope, empowerment, and wisdom with those around me that go beyond RDM. As leaders and caregivers, our eyes must stay open and attentive to seeing God's movement and God's invitation for us to join in this sacred work. Attending to the extraordinary in the mundane experience requires a centeredness that comes from a rested soul and body.

The Quest for Authentic Connection: A Life's Work of Rest and Nurturing Relationships

Caregivers and leaders need to be fed and replenished so we have the strength and inner space to carry on our work with consistent quality. Unfortunately, seeking this replenishment has not always come easy for me. Knowing the necessity of rest and self-care has not automatically made its way into my priorities. Too often, like some of RDM's SGKA clients, I need reminders to break the false connection between my sense of worth and my success in performances and achievements. We, as givers of care, must continue to learn how to rest and focus on self-care if we are to advocate for marginalized persons and counsel others in need. Grace Kim reminds us that "'rest' in the biblical texts is a profoundly spiritual term, having to do with inner peace, assurance and hope . . . In order for them to go out and make a difference in their lives and the lives of their sisters, they first need to rest."[19] Without rest, our own toxicity could seep through, adding more injury than care to the ones who come seeking help. Rest can help us remain grounded in the complexity of who we are and make available within us the room to care for other human beings in their complexities. Taking time to rest and reconnect with our own souls and our Creator allows us to foster authentic connections with others.

Caregivers of complex hybrid populations need genuine, safe, and nurturing relationships and friendships that allow them to be free to be themselves. In my own journey with RDM, from its inception to the years of giving care, I have found the crucial need of places where I could unload, people to whom I could talk to about anything without fear of judgment or negative consequences. One of the largest sources of pain for me is the loneliness, multiple misunderstandings, and projections others have placed upon me as

19. Kim, *Grace of Sophia*, 149.

Opening the Red Door

I stand in in-between spaces. Too often I have felt overwhelmed with expectations from my clients or congregation members. Many have assumed that as a leader, I must be spiritually astute, strong, and intelligent and must act in certain prescribed ways that are expected of a female pastor and caregiver.

Through my relationships with a spiritual director and close friends outside of RDM and the church, I have found spaces that give me the freedom to play and work out my thoughts, feelings, and needs, allowing me to learn and to accept myself as a flawed human being. In such spaces, I feel safe to imagine and dream of other potential, third spaces. All caregivers and community leaders need free and safe spaces where they can be accepted as their true selves so that creative spaces can open within them that can bring about empowering transformations.

Going Beyond the Red Door Ministry

The results of my study show that a third space that encourages personal transformation leads people with hybrid identities and cultures to live more meaningful and renewed lives. Their transformation is multiplied when they empower others toward freedom and agency. The abundance of life I hope for SGKAs and other marginalized groups starts with my own rich relationship with God, others, and self. RDM has been the fruitful harvest of these relationships. This counseling ministry has served as one example of a space that encourages growth, healing, wholeness, hope, empowerment, and wisdom. I conclude this book having more questions about how more spaces like RDM can be formed for the Korean American community and other marginalized groups.

What elements are needed to create larger spaces that bring intergenerational communities together to work across cultural difference to spur communal and institutional change? What is the role of the church in forging intergenerational spaces where transformation of self and other are fueled? How can marginalized populations find home and acceptance in carefully crafted spaces that are mindful of theological exploration, cultural difference, postcolonial theory, and context-specific pastoral needs? How can SGKAs who are nurtured in a carefully crafted space co-create new centers that will impact the lives of successive generations who will one day inhabit new challenges in their community, nation, and world?

Appendix

Interview Questions

How did you hear about Red Door Ministry?

What brought you to Red Door Ministry?

How would you describe what happens in Red Door Ministry?

    Is there an image or metaphor that comes to mind?

What impact, if any, has Red Door Ministry had on your mental health?

What impact, if any, has Red Door Ministry had in how you understand yourself and the world around you?

What are the positives and negatives you have experienced from coming into this space?

Have you had counseling before? If so, please describe . . .

    If so, is you experience here different from previous counseling experiences?

    If not, how does/did your experience of Red Door Ministry compare to what you imagine counseling to be?

Appendix

Has your participation in Red Door Ministry changed understandings of God/faith/religion?

> If so, How?

What elements or factors would you say has been the most important in your process here?

In terms of your self-understanding and relationships with others, what are your hopes?

Do you feel more empowered in your life as a result of coming to Red Door Ministry?

> If so, what might have contributed to you feeling this way?

> If not, explain why not.

Do you identify as a SGKA (Second-generation Korean American)? If so, please describe your experience.

> One way to describe your experience may be to answer this question: What does a day look like for you as a SGKA?

Has your time at Red Door Ministry had any impact on how you view yourself as a second-generation Korean American in the dominant (white, non-white) culture? If so, how?

Given this research will be published, what wisdom from your own experience would you offer other SGKAs.

Additional Questions for the second interview after summaries and themes were pulled from the first interview.

Any new insights about your process in Red Door Ministry?

What themes might I have overlooked?

What did I get wrong in your summary?

What needs more focus or emphasis?

Interview Questions

What might improve your experience in Red Door Ministry?

What might be missing in your experience of Red Door Ministry?

Bibliography

Alvarez, Alvin. *Asian American Psychology Current Perspectives*. New York: Psychology, 2009.
Baker, Don. *Korean Spirituality*. Dimensions of Asian Spirituality. Honolulu: University of Hawaii Press, 2008.
Balingit, Moriah, Hannah Natanson and Yutao Chen. "As Schools Reopen, Asian American Students are Missing from Classrooms," *The Washington Post* (March 4, 2021). https://www.washingtonpost.com/education/asian-american-students-home-school-in-person-pandemic/2021/03/02/eb7056bc-7786-11eb-8115-9ad5e9c02117_story.html.
Bhabha, Homi K. *The Location of Culture*. London: Routledge, 2004.
———. "On Writing Rights." In *Globalizing Rights: The Oxford Amnesty Lectures 1999*, edited by Matthew J. Gibney, 162–83. Oxford: Oxford University Press, 2003.
Boff, Leonard. *Essential Care: An Ethics of Human Nature*. Waco, TX: Baylor University Press, 2008.
Bollas, Christopher. "A Theory for the True Self." In *Winnicott and the Psychoanalytic Tradition: Interpretation and Other Psychoanalytic Issues*, edited by Lesley Caldwell, 21–43. London: Routledge, 2007.
———. "The Aesthetic Moment and the Search for Transformation." In *Transitional Objects and Potential Spaces: Literary Uses of D. W. Winnicott*, edited by Peter L. Rudnytsky, 40–49. New York: Columbia University Press, 1994.
Brock, Rita Nakashima, et al. eds. *Off the Menu: Asian and Asian North American Women's Religion and Theology*. Louisville, KY: Westminster John Knox, 2007.
Capps, Donald. *Agents of Hope: A Pastoral Psychology*. Eugene, OR: Wipf & Stock, 2001.
———. *The Depleted Self: Sin in a Narcissistic Age*. Minneapolis: Fortress, 1993.
Carter, Robert T. *The Influence of Race and Racial Identity in Psychotherapy: Toward a Racially Inclusive Model*. New York: Wiley, 1995.
Cheah, Joseph, and Grace Ji-Sun Kim. *Theological Reflections on "Gangnam Style": A Racial, Sexual, and Cultural Critique*. New York: Palgrave Macmillan, 2014.

Bibliography

Choi, Hee An. A *Postcolonial Self: Korean Immigrant Theology and Church*. Albany: State University of New York Press, 2016.

Choi, Namkee G. *Psychosocial Aspects of the Asian-American Experience: Diversity Within Diversity*. New York: Routledge, 2001.

Chong, Kelly H. "What it Means to be Christian: The Role of Religion in the Construction of Ethnic Identity and Boundary Among Second-Generation Korean Americans." *Sociology of Religion* 59 no. 3 (September 21, 1998) 259–86.

Chung, Brenda. "Growing up Korean American: Navigating a Complex Search for Belonging." In *Younger Generation Korean Experiences in the United States: Personal Narratives on Ethnic and Racial Identities*, edited by Pyong Gap Min and Thomas Chung, 77–87. New York: Lexington, 2014.

Cooper-White, Pamela. *Many Voices: Pastoral Psychotherapy in Relational and Theological Perspective*. Minneapolis: Fortress, 2007.

Creswell, John W. *Research Design: Qualitative, Quantitative, and Mixed Methods Approaches*. Thousand Oaks, CA: Sage, 2003.

Denzin, Norman K., and Yvonna S. Lincoln. *The Landscape of Qualitative Research: Theories and Issues*. Thousand Oaks, CA: Sage, 1998.

Du Bois, W. E. B. *The Souls of Black Folk*. Oxford: Oxford University Press, 2007.

Fausset, Richard and Neil Vigdor. "8 People Killed in Atlanta-Area Massage Parlor Shootings." *The New York Times*, (March 16, 2021). https://www.nytimes.com/2021/03/16/us/atlanta-shootings-massage-parlor.html

Fiddes, Paul S. *Participating in God: A Pastoral Doctrine of the Trinity*. Louisville, KY: Westminster John Knox, 2000.

Fong, Rowena. *Culturally Competent Practice with Immigrant and Refugee Children and Families*. New York: Guilford, 2004.

Fong, Timothy P. *Asian Americans: Experiences and Perspectives*. Upper Saddle River, NJ: Prentice Hall, 2000.

Freire, Paulo. *Pedagogy of Hope: Reliving Pedagogy of the Oppressed*. London: Bloomsbury Academic, 2014.

Green, Andre. *Play and Reflection in Donald Winnicott's Writings*. London: Karnac, 2005.

Hall, Gordon C. Nagayama. "Culture-Specific Ecological Models of Asian American Violence." In *Asian American Psychology: The Science of Lives in Context*, edited by Gordon C. Nagayama Hall and Sumie Okazaki, 153–70. Washington, DC: American Psychological Association, 2002.

Hearn, Mark Chung. *Religious Experience Among Second Generation Korean Americans*. New York: Palgrave Macmillan, 2016.

Hertig, Young Lee. *Cultural Tug of War: The Korean Immigrant Family and Church in Transition*. Nashville: Abingdon, 2001.

Hong, Christine J. *Identity, Youth, and Gender in the Korean American Church*. New York: Palgrave Macmillan, 2015.

hooks, bell. *Feminist Theory: From Margin to Center*. London: Pluto, 2000.

Huddart, David. *Homi K. Bhabha*. London: Routledge, 2006.

Hurley, Michael. "Who's on Whose Margins?" In *Researching the Margins: Strategies for Ethical and Rigorous Research with Marginalised Communities*, edited by Marian Pitts and Anthony Smith, 160–87. Basingstoke, UK: Palgrave Macmillan, 2007.

Jacobi, Jolande. *The Psychology of Jung: An Introduction with Illustrations*. New Haven: Yale University Press, 1943.

Bibliography

Jefferson, Thomas. "Declaration of Independence," *National Archives* (July 1776). https://www.archives.gov/founding-docs/declaration-transcript

Jeung, Russell. *Faithful Generations Race and New Asian American Churches*. New Brunswick, NJ: Rutgers University Press, 2005.

Joh, Wonhee Anne. *Heart of the Cross: A Postcolonial Christology*. Louisville, KY: Westminster John Knox Press, 2006.

———. "Violence and Asian American Experience: From Abjection to Jeong." In *Off the Menu: Asian and Asian North American Women's Religion and Theology*, edited by Rita Nakashima Brock, et al., 145–63. Louisville, KY: Westminster John Knox, 2007.

Jung, Carl Gustav. *Man and His Symbols*. New York: Dell, 1978.

———. *Memories, Dreams, Reflections*. New York: Vintage, 1989.

———. *Psyche and Symbol: A Selection from the Writings of C.G. Jung*. Princeton, NJ: Princeton University Press, 1991.

———. *The Undiscovered Self*. New York: Signet, 2006.

Kang, Byung Moon, and Cameron Lee. "Differentiation of Self and Generational Differences in the Korean Immigrant Church." *Journal of Family Ministry* 14 no. 4 (December 1, 2000) 22–31.

Kang, Hyeyoung, et al. "Redeeming Immigrant Parents: How Korean American Emerging Adults Reinterpret Their Childhood." *Journal of Adolescent Research* 25 no. 3 (May 1, 2010) 441–64.

Kang, S. Steve. *Unveiling the Socioculturally Constructed Multivoiced Self: Themes of Self Construction and Self Integration in the Narratives of Second-Generation Korean American Young Adults*. Lanham, MD: University Press of America, 2002.

Kibria, Nazli. *Becoming Asian American: Second-Generation Chinese and Korean American Identities*. Baltimore, MD: Johns Hopkins University Press, 2002.

Kim, Dae Young. *Second-Generation Korean Americans the Struggle for Full Inclusion*. The New Americans: Recent Immigration and American Society. El Paso, TX: LFB Scholarly, 2013.

Kim, Eunjung. "Korean American Parents' Reconstruction of Immigrant Parenting in the United States." *Journal of Cultural Diversity* 19 no. 4 (2012).

Kim, Grace Ji-Sun. *Embracing the Other: The Transformative Spirit of Love*. Grand Rapids: Eerdmans, 2015.

———. *The Grace of Sophia: A Korean North American Women's Christology*. Cleveland, OH: Pilgrim, 2002.

———. *The Holy Spirit, Chi, and the Other: A Model of Global and Intercultural Pneumatology*. New York: Palgrave Macmillan, 2011.

Kim, Kwang Chung, Won Moo Hurh, and Shin Kim. "Generation Differences in Korean Immigrants' Life Conditions in the United States." *Sociological Perspectives* 36 no. 3 (1993).

Kim, Nadia and Christine Oh. "On Being a 'Successful Failure': Korean-American Students and the Structural-Cultural Paradox." In *Second-Generation Korean Experiences in the United States and Canada*, edited by Pyong Gap Min and Samuel Noh. 160–85 Lanham, MD: Lexington, 2014.

Kim, Nami. "The 'Indigestible' Asian: The Unifying Term 'Asian' in Theological Discourse" in *Off the Menu: Asian and Asian North American Women's Religion and Theology*, edited by Rita Nakashima Brock et al., 23–43. Louisville, KY: Westminster John Knox, 2007.

Bibliography

Kim, Rebecca Y. *God's New Whiz Kids? Korean American Evangelicals on Campus*. New York: New York University Press, 2006.

Kim, Sharon. *A Faith of Our Own: Second-Generation Spirituality in Korean American Churches*. New Brunswick, NJ: Rutgers University Press, 2010.

Kwon, Ho Youn, et al. *Korean Americans and Their Religions: Pilgrims and Missionaries from a Different Shore*. University Park, PA: Pennsylvania State University Press, 2001.

Kvale, Steinar. *InterViews: Learning the Craft of Qualitative Research Interviewing*. Los Angeles: Sage, 2015.

Lartey, Emmanuel Y. *In Living Color: An Intercultural Approach to Pastoral Care and Counseling*. London: Jessica Kingsley, 2003.

———. *Pastoral Theology in an Intercultural World*. Peterborough UK: Epworth, 2006.

———. *Postcolonializing God: An African Practical Theology*. London: SCM, 2013.

———. "Postcolonializing Pastoral Theology: Enhancing the Intercultural Paradigm." In *Pastoral Theology and Care: Critical Trajectories in Theory and Practice*, edited by Nancy J. Ramsay, 79–97. Chichester, UK: Wiley-Blackwell, 2018.

Lee, Courtland C. *Multicultural Issues in Counseling: New Approach to Diversity*. Alexandria, VA: American Counseling Association, 2013.

Lee, Helene. "*Miyeok Guk* for the Korean Soul." In *Younger-Generation Korean Experiences in the United States: Personal Narratives on Ethnic and Racial Identities*, edited by Pyong Gap Min and Thomas Chung, 133–44. Lanham, MD: Lexington, 2014.

Lee, Sang Hyun. *From a Liminal Place: An Asian American Theology*. Minneapolis: Fortress, 2010.

Leong, Frederick T. L. *Handbook of Asian American Psychology*. Thousand Oaks, CA: Sage, 2007.

Levin, Sam. "'We're the Geeks, the Prostitutes': Asian American Actors on Hollywood's Barriers." *The Guardian* (April 11, 2017). http://www.theguardian.com/world/2017/apr/11/asian-american-actors-whitewashing-hollywood.

Lifton, Robert Jay. *The Protean Self: Human Resilience in an Age of Fragmentation*. New York: Basic, 1993.

Maddux, W. W. et al. "When Being a Model Minority is Good . . . and Bad: Realistic Threat Explains Negativity toward Asian Americans." *Personality and Social Psychology Bulletin*, 34(1), 2008.

McClure, Barbara J. *Moving Beyond Individualism in Pastoral Care and Counseling: Reflections on Theory, Theology, and Practice*. Eugene, OR: Wipf & Stock 2010.

McGoldrick, Monica, and Kenneth V. Hardy, eds. *Re-Visioning Family Therapy: Race, Culture, and Gender in Clinical Practice*. 2nd ed. New York: Guilford, 2008.

Min, Pyong Gap, ed. *Koreans in North America: Their Twenty-First Century Experiences*. Lanham, MD: Lexington, 2013.

———, ed. *Second Generation: Ethnic Identity Among Asian Americans*. Walnut Creek, CA: AltaMira, 2002.

Min, Pyong Gap, and Rose Kim, eds. *Struggle for Ethnic Identity: Narratives by Asian American Professionals*. Critical perspectives on Asian Pacific Americans series 4. Walnut Creek, CA: AltaMira, 1999.

Moon, Hellena. "The 'Living Human Web' Revisited: An Asian American Pastoral Care and Counseling Perspective." *Sacred Spaces: The e-Journal of the American Association of Pastoral Counselors* 3 (2011) 14–43.

Bibliography

Okagaki, Lynn and Kathryn E. Bojczyk. "Perspectives on Asian American Development." in *Asian American Psychology: The Science of Lives in Context* edited by Gordon C. Nagayama Hall and Sumie Okazaki, 67–104. Washington DC: American Psychological Association, 2002.

Ogden, Thomas. "On Holding and Containing, Being and Dreaming." In *Winnicott and the Psychoanalytic Tradition: Interpretation and Other Psychoanalytic Issues*, edited by Lesley Caldwell, 117–46. London; New York: Karnac, 2007.

Oh, David C. *Second-Generation Korean Americans and Transnational Media: Diasporic Identifications*. Lanham, MD: Lexington, 2015.

Palmer, Parker J. *A Hidden Wholeness: The Journey Toward an Undivided Life: Welcoming the Soul and Weaving Community in a Wounded World*. San Francisco: Jossey-Bass, 2004.

Papero, Daniel V. *Bowen Family Systems Theory*. Boston: Allyn and Bacon, 1990.

Paris, Django, and Maisha Winn. *Humanizing Research: Decolonizing Qualitative Inquiry with Youth and Communities*. Thousand Oaks, CA: Sage, 2014.

Park, Andrew Sung. *From Hurt to Healing: A Theology of the Wounded*. Nashville: Abingdon, 2004.

———. *Racial Conflict and Healing: An Asian-American Theological Perspective*. Eugene, OR: Wipf & Stock, 2009.

Park, Sophia. "Pastoral Care for the 1.5 Generation: In-Between Space as the 'New' Cultural Space." In *Women Out of Order: Risking Change and Creating Care in a Multicultural World*, edited by Jeanne Stevenson Moessner and Teresa Snorton, 230–242. Minneapolis: Fortress, 2010.

Pattison, Stephen. *Shame Theory, Therapy, Theology*. Cambridge: Cambridge University Press, 2000.

Phan, Peter C. *Christianity with an Asian Face: Asian American Theology in the Making*. Maryknoll, NY: Orbis, 2003.

Ramsay, Nancy J. "Contemporary Pastoral Theology: A Wider Vision for the Practice of Love." In *Pastoral Care and Counseling: Redefining the Paradigms*, edited by Nancy J. Ramsay, 155–76. Nashville: Abingdon, 2004.

Rhee, Siyon. "The Impact of Immigration and Acculturation on the Mental Health of Asian Americans."In *Handbook of Mental Health and Acculturation in Asian American Families* edited by Nhi-Ha Trinh. 89–110. New York: Humana, 2009.

Rudnytsky, Peter L., ed. *Transitional Objects and Potential Spaces: Literary Uses of D. W. Winnicott*. New York: Columbia University Press, 1994.

Said, Edward W. *Orientalism*. New York: Vintage, 1979.

Schwartz, M. M. "Introduction: D. W. Winnicott's Cultural Space." *Psychoanalytic Review* (1992) 169–74.

Seeley, Karen M. *Cultural Psychotherapy: Working with Culture in the Clinical Encounter*. Northvale, NJ: Jason Aronson, 1999.

Seol, Kyoung Ok, and Richard M. Lee. "The Effects of Religious Socialization and Religious Identity on Psychosocial Functioning in Korean American Adolescents from Immigrant Families." *Journal of Family Psychology* 26 no. 3 (June 2012) 371–80.

Sharp, Melinda A. McGarrah. *Misunderstanding Stories: Toward a Postcolonial Pastoral Theology*. Eugene, OR: Wipf & Stock, 2013.

Smith, Hayley. " Anti-Asian Hate Crimes have Spiked in Cities around the U.S., Study Finds." *Los Angeles Times* (May 4, 2021). https://www.latimes.com/california/story/2021-25-04/anti-asian-hate-crimes-spike-us-cities-study-finds.

Bibliography

Sollod, Robert N., and Christopher F. Monte. *Beneath the Mask: An Introduction to Theories of Personality*. Hoboken, NJ: Wiley, 2008.

Son, Chul Woo. *The Motives of Self-Sacrifice in Korean American Culture, Family, and Marriage: From Filial Piety to Familial Integrity*. Eugene, OR: Wipf & Stock, 2013.

Spickard, Paul. *Almost All Aliens: Immigration, Race, and Colonialism in American History and Identity*. New York: Routledge, 2007.

Stevenson, Leslie, et al. *Twelve Theories of Human Nature*. 6th ed. Oxford: Oxford University Press, 2012.

Sue, Derald Wing, and David Sue. *Counseling the Culturally Diverse: Theory and Practice*. Hoboken, NJ: Wiley, 2015.

Tseng, Viva et al. "Asian Americans' Education Experiences." In *Handbook of Asian American Psychology*. edited by Frederick T. L. Leong, 105–23. Thousand Oaks, CA: Sage, 2007

Tuan, Mia. "Second Generation Asian American Identity: Clues from the Asian Ethnic Experience." In *Second Generation: Ethnic Identity Among Asian Americans*. edited by Pyong Gap Min, 209–37. Walnut Creek, CA: AltaMira, 2002.

Winnicott, D. W. *Human Nature*. Bristol, PA: Brunner/Mazel, 1988.

———. "The Location of Cultural Experience." In *Playing and Reality*. D.W. Winnicott, 128–39. London: Routledge, 2005.

———."Playing: Creative Activity and the Search for the Self," In *Playing and Reality*. D.W. Winnicott, 71–86. London: Routledge, 2005.

———."Playing: A Theoretical Statement." In *Playing and Reality*. D.W. Winnicott, 51–70. London: Routledge, 2005.

———."Transitional Objects and Transitional Phenomena." In *Playing and Reality*. D.W. Winnicott, 1–34. London: Routledge, 2005.

Westervelt, Eric. "Anger and Fear as Asian American Seniors Targeted in Bay Area Attacks," *NPR*, (February 12, 2021). https://www.npr.org/2021/02/12/966940217/anger-and-fear-as-asian-american-seniors-targeted-in-bay-area-attacks.

Warner, R. Stephen. "The Korean Immigrant Church as Case and Model." In *Korean Americans and Their Religions: Pilgrims and Missionaries from a Different Shore*, edited by Ho-Youn Kwon et al., 25–52. University Park, PA: Pennsylvania State University Press, 2001.

Wong, Sandra. "Depression Level in Inner-City Asian American Adolescents: The Contributions of Cultural Orientation and Interpersonal Relationships." In *Psychosocial Aspect of the Asian-American Experience: Diversity within Diversity*, edited by Namkee G. Choi, 49–64. New York: Routledge, 2001.

Wong, William. *Yellow Journalist Dispatches from Asian America*: Philadelphia: Temple University Press, 2010.

Yeomans, Curt. "Gwinnett a Large Draw for Koreans in Georgia." *Gwinnett Dailhy Post.com* (April 2016). http://www.gwinnettdailypost.com/local/gwinnett-a-large-draw-for-koreans-in-georgia/article_02338702-b0a7-56af-9dbd-355dfofd17ac.html.

Yoo, Grace J. *Caring Across Generations: The Linked Lives of Korean American Families*. New York: New York University Press, 2014.

Yoo, Paula. *Good Enough*. New York: HarperTeen, 2008.

Young, Jacob Yongseok. *Korean, Asian, or American?: The Identity, Ethnicity, and Autobiography of Second-Generation Korean American Christians*. Lanham MD: University Press of America, 2012.

Index

1.5 generation, 61–62

Asian hate crimes, 23
authenticity, 65–67, 149

Bhabha, Homi, 46–51, 65

Capps, Donald, 73–76
center, 3, 114–16, 117–18, 122–36, 139–41
chi, 48–49, 131–32
colonialism, 21, 44–45, 50–51, 66–67
Confucian values, 17–19, 29, 37, 81
creativity, 46, 54–56, 82–83, 86–87, 100, 103–4, 123, 136
culture, 14, 16–20, 29 46, 48, 50–52, 61–64, 71–72, 81, 103–8, 145–46

divine dance, 110–14, 123–24, 126, 131, 136
double life, 14–24, 34–39, 148
Du Bois, W.E.B, 15, 39

empowerment (see power)

family, 11, 17–19, 24–25, 29–32, 68–69, 80–82

first-generation Korean American, 13, 19–20, 24, 26–27, 29–30, 36–37, 134
freedom, 20, 43–44, 91–92, 119–20, 128, 135–36,
fusion chef, 102–7, 108, 109

gender, 37–39, 78–82
guilt, 31–32, 76

Hahn, 99–102, 106–8, 141–42
home, 11–12, 14, 17–19, 24, 30–32, 35–36, 40, 68–69, 128, 130
holding environment, 57–58
hooks, bell, 67, 118, 127
hope, 74, 124, 132–33, 139, 145
hybridity, 50–52, 96, 103–4, 131–32, 145–46, 147

individualism, 71–72

jeong, 96–99, 128–30, 141
Joh, Woonhee, 96–97, 115, 141
Jung, Carl, 89–94, 95

Kim, Grace Jisun, 44, 49–50, 81, 103, 108, 122, 127, 131–32, 149
Kim, Sharon, 16, 147

Index

Korean-American church, 12, 16, 34–39, 53–54, 63–64, 108–9, 116, 147–48
Korean-American Dream, 13, 25–27, 31–32, 36, 39, 76–77

Lartey, Emmanuel, 7, 46–47, 49, 59, 111

margins, 3, 7, 111–12, 114–18, 122–24, 126–28
Min, Pyong Gap, 8, 15
model minority, 27–28, 31, 48

oppression, 6–7, 34–39, 45, 47, 75, 114–17, 124–30, 143

Park, Andrew, 75–76, 99–102, 118
Park, Sophia, 61
Pattison, Stephen, 74–76, 80, 84, 87
pastoral theology, 4, 44, 111
perpetual foreigner, 12, 22–24, 45
play, 54–56, 86–89, 146
postcolonialism, 6–7, 43–44, 46–51, 96, 145–47
potential space, 54–56, 86–88
power, 30–31, 43–44, 48, 96–99, 114–15, 124, 126–30, 132–34, 136, 139–43

protean self, 39–40

racism, 21–24, 26, 27–28, 30–31, 35, 45, 96
rest, 121, 135, 149

sacrifice, 26, 31, 38
Said, Edward, 44–46
self-exploration, 89–92
sexism, 38, 45, 96
shadow, 92–94
shame, 31–34, 72–82, 84–85, 87, 90–91, 93, 97–98, 101, 104, 107–9
stereotype, 27, 47, 59

third space, 9, 50–52, 145–48
transitional object, 56–58, 83–85
true self, 65–66, 83, 86–88

violence, 21, 29–31

wholeness, 39–40, 89, 100–101
Winnicott, Donald, 54, 56, 57–58, 82–89, 94–95
woori, 72

www.ingramcontent.com/pod-product-compliance
Lightning Source LLC
Chambersburg PA
CBHW050819160426
43192CB00010B/1816